Meanderings

The Journey of Seeking My Soul

WHO AM I?

Meanderings

The Journey of Seeking My Soul
WHO AM I?

IRENA ISIS STEININGER

EXCELLER BOOKS®
A GLOBAL PRESS

Dedication

I dedicate this book to my Human brethren, especially those in female embodiment – to my ancestors on whose shoulders I stand – to the boundless choices we're given to explore, experience, play on this grand world stage – to my many nobly human teachers and guides – to the ONE creating Spirit, the Cosmic Mind exploring HerSelf through each one of Her HUman children – to Her Grace, forgiveness, and compassion – to Life itself, so bountiful, challenging, beautiful... I bow to ALL!

This book is dedicated to the Divine Wisdom, Truth, and Light that can never perish – to CosMahaDeviji – to the ONE lovelight that glows in us all, eternally!

Acknowledgment

My gratitude goes out to all forces that played a major role in my search for my own true self: Cosmic and Earth Mothers, forces of light contrasting darkness. The all-encompassing coherence of cosmic love... my family as my greatest challenge, the "petty tyrants" I stumbled over, the many fellow travellers who inspired and fired me... my own intrinsic, self-freeing Spirit driving me on to meet my Self... my supportive publishers, who carry my story out for the benefit of people in this time of grand global transformation – may it encourage all to seek their own divine unfolding...

Thank you!

Table of Contents

Introduction –
Why Am I Sharing My Life Journey?

Sharing insights drawn from personal experiences deeply resonates with people. My struggles, desires, mistakes, failures, dark thoughts, tears, laughter, joys, triumphs, and ecstasies, along with some of my insights and humour, belong to everyone.

I explore the power of Words of Truth as a supreme expressive, inspirational, and transformative tool in the world and my understanding. As I am writing, the various stages and stations of my life pass by my inner eye/space, and I am delighted to realize that the way I perceive and express my life experiences has changed profoundly. My view of it all has taken a very different perspective! Wow, this feels good; it makes me realize just how I have shifted internally – and I am grateful, ever so grateful, that so much healing has now taken place at long, long last, after so much struggle and more thwarted efforts! My mind had been so full of shit, and it has greatly diminished! Cognitions of truth shall fill the void exclusively.

For a while, I thought that my life journey had been unique and unusual. Well, unique it may be, but unusual? I have encountered countless fellow travelers on different levels of being—seekers like myself, individuals yearning for life's deeper meaning and greater possibilities, and even those who ultimately come to realize that even they need to heal. Life becomes so much richer when we share our individual stories, intricately woven by hands far greater than our own.

What motivated my life quest to move around was the fact that I felt painfully alien in the world that I had landed myself in – post-war Germany. I felt like a stranger there, and as much as I tried in the course of my life, I did not find my place in that society. The Western life design altogether seemed strangely uprooted, sickly distorted, one great big LIE! And this ugly white skin!!! It was everything BUT "my" world within, and this was the motor that drove me out and about.

I set out to seek a healthy and fulfilled life as I knew it faintly, somewhere deep down in my inner world. Seeking a paradise as my inner world remembered it, even if only vaguely. Western life appeared desperately in need of healing, reordering, balancing, appeasing, and cleansing as it was so everything BUT healthy and happy. It was completely upside down to me.

Unexpectedly, along my journey, I unearthed forgotten and buried fragments of my soul, slowly uncovering my own healing and transformation. Through this process, I began to recreate myself as my inner and outer worlds continuously reflected and inspired one another.

My path unfolded like a river winding through the landscapes of the inner and outer worlds. Yet, nothing from the outer world ever settled permanently on its banks—no husband, no children, no house or material assets, no title, career, or overflowing bank account. Nothing tangible remained with me, nothing to define me in the mundane world we inhabit. All I carried was the flowing river of my journey, moving steadily toward its destined source—the vast, infinite OCEAN! I AM A NOMAD! Eternally!

But, time and again, my travelling canoe gets delayed or sucked into muddy waters, ya swamps, and they yield: tons of experiences! Therein, I am a millionaire!

The planets had blessed me with plenty of radiant and powerful fire energy, yes. Due to Jupiter's ever-itching travelling leg, I need to move around and find the expansion of mind and insights through experiences – meeting myself in the mirror of the other, the "strange". An overgenerous Mercurian kiss of mental overload made me a true "space cadet". But – oh gratitude – they had also laid some "sleeping policemen" into my path, Saturnian speedbumps, so that I slow down, be grounded and get REAL! And Leo, as my rising sign, is responsible for my creativity needing to be expressed in so many different ways.

And for radiating Her Majesty, yes, I wanna shine – from the inside out – Divine!

Except for the universal and foreseeable stages we all travel through from birth to death, there is no pattern or order in that meandering, at least not tangible, for long years.

So – be ready for a bumpy ride in a 4-wheel-drive through rough terrain! Or a roller coaster? – No, not really that dramatic! You decide!

Actually, I want to share the highlights/insights rather than the swampy sticky-stuck experiences, yet only together can we make that unique design my life – any life - creates. There is no saint without a past, as there is no sinner without a future. Truth is truth, and to make this a complete work of sharing the internal aspects of my journey, I need to at least touch upon the sticky stuff also – with the sole intention of encouraging the readers themselves to beware of the burden of their own swampy shadows hidden even to themselves, but integratable by keen awareness and truthful cognition any time! There is no one among us who does not have an issue somewhere deep within, buried away in hiding, denied, but painfully there, a cancerous burden, operating under obscure cover – until liberated into the light.

The river of my life – much as the great winding snake of the Amazon in Brazil – has hundreds of side arms, and I invariably get lost in its labyrinth until I make that liberating choice of faith!

Enjoy the poems and photos that serve to illustrate my various stations and add some sensual, visual and feeling inspiration.

Ultimately, my story is just one more example of how Spirit or CosMa expresses itself through us, seeking to experience and delight in its own essence.

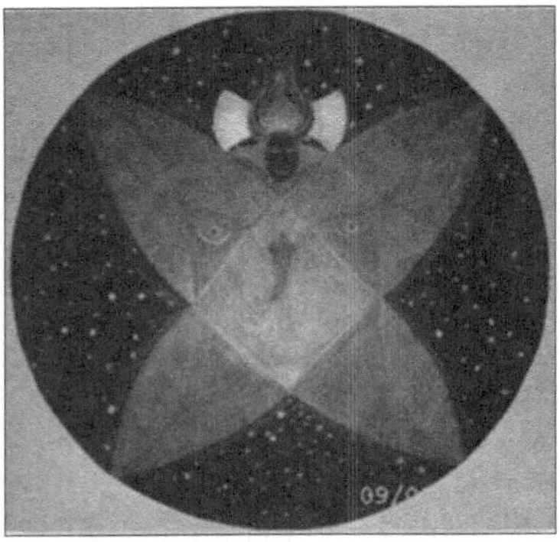

CosMa, One of My Art Works

Landing in a Cuckoo's Nest

Paradoxically – I felt like a stranger when I landed myself in this world: de-va(war)-stated Germany, a tiny village along the river Sieg near the Rhine, living in a house that was surrounded by a huge potato field with chickens populating the garden and a giant sewage pit. All the neighbors were farmers, and life was simple and sweet for me then.

My father is a good-natured gentleman who expects his family to function according to his unspoken rules, thus supporting his career, which in turn supports us all. My Mom was an attractive, slim, slender, sporty lady who loved to dance and make merry. She had a lot of zest in her. Born a double Capricorn, she also carried tons of fears. I experience her as tense, frustrated, negative, irrational, unpredictable – and very conform = polite, well-mannered, discreet and well-presentable to any outsider. They loved each other somehow, as far as that is possible where the man is the undoubtable master of the house… more appropriate to call it a good match!

The village we lived in was the home to my mother, who married this handsome pilot stationed in her village during the war. He was lucky he did not get shot down to die while killing the British as a night bomber pilot, as many of his companions did. He was a Bavarian from a "good family", all highly educated and holding responsible posts in a small town in Northern Bavaria.

At the age of 13, he learnt to fly gliders, those silent wooden birds that sail on the wind's mercy once they are pulled up into the air. Flying planes became his passion, and after World War II, he was able to link his passion with an interesting profession, that of an aviation psychologist with the task of setting up a psychology section in the German Research Institute for Aviation and Space Travel, in close collaboration with Lufthansa. Against all expectations, as the first of its kind worldwide, this institute developed into a great success for my father. Thus, I experienced him as a busy but settled, creative, inventive, and fulfilled person who was responsible for both the calling of his career and the demands of the family. He is, in fact, a loyal family man and father always. He expects us to function as smooth wheels in his little family while simultaneously being caring, empathetic, and humorous when dealing with us. The ingenious Cancer/Sagittarius combination had kissed him at his birth time. Our home is ever filled with interesting folk, world travelers, pilots, for innumerous occasions to get together and enjoy. Dad is a well-loved friend, guide and teacher to many.

I deeply love, admire, and bond with him more than I do with my mother. I feel at home in his mother's big house in Bavaria, where we spend all our long summer holidays in the large circle of family. There is a kind of order and, consequently, some sense of safety I feel in the lap of that large family. I discovered the family emblem in this house, which goes back 500 years into the past and depicts a knight holding a stone in his right hand. The meaning of this emblem and the family name is: "Keeper of the Stone of Strength and Power." The founding father is set in stone in the small Austrian town of Braunau/Inn forever as one representing strength and power, and he was elevated to the status of aristocracy because of his excellence.

Pride fills me upon learning this and an inner calling to stand up to this name and its meaning. With my name Irene, meaning peace, added, my full name thus reads: "Peaceful carrier of the stone of strength and power." I have been working on it ever since.

My Dad's family carries some ethics that resonate with me, and I observe them keenly. One of my uncles would assemble us children on our beds at night and tell us stories. He had been a

Don Kossak during the war and was full of interesting lore. The other uncle, a country doctor with a VW beetle travelling the countryside serving those stashed away in remote villages, is full of playful mischief and a delight to me, yet he is also very straight and strict, and I love him for his limitless humorous pranks AND the clarity he conveys.

My aunt is a piano teacher. She suffered quite a fate by coming home pregnant and unmarried during wartime. Her mother, my grandmother, would not have that kind of thing under her roof, and she was simply banned from the house for many years. So, she had to raise her daughter alone and must have gone through very rough and tough times. But she is the gentlest, kindest, most caring and loving human around. She always carried a smile full of goodness, and she WAS pure goodness. I felt connected to her in my later years when I understood her much deeper. I do not know how she was reconciled to the family, but she was. The other aunt remained unmarried for different reasons. She took care of my grandmother, which was challenging since she was a hard-hearted and stubborn old lady. She, too, had gone through a lot, giving birth to 9 children, losing 2, experiencing two World wars, losing two sons to it and at 50, she lost her husband, a busy lawyer, to cancer. This all is Dad's family. She would line up all her seven offspring regularly and give them a solid spanking, as is mentioned in the bible: a father who beats his son is a good father??? She had plenty of servants to help her manage it all well. People were made of different materials in those days. She was born in 1884!

My mother is from a simple family. The war brought my parents together, as my father, a bomber pilot, was stationed in the tiny town of her origin, where she happened to be the secretary in the large and beautiful Cure House, where the pilots were accommodated. It was love at first sight, as my father narrated, infatuation, I would say, as he added that she was really sexy, and then he blushed at revealing something so intimate to his children; cute, isn't it? Anyhow, they did match somehow, and got married in 1948, after the war and when my father had nearly completed his studies.

My mother had a natural talent for sports and a deep love for it. She also adored dancing and often dreamed of elegant clothes, sparkling jewelry, and playing the role of a glamorous diva. Truth be told, she was not the kind of woman who should have settled for marriage and motherhood; she was meant for a life of her own, chasing ambitions and forging a career. But life had other plans. She did get married, and I became her first child.

From the very start, our relationship was a kind of tug-of-war. Even before I was born, we seemed to be at odds. When she was pregnant with me, she was so small that the nurses initially sent her home, telling her it wasn't time yet. But my mother, stubborn and determined as ever, insisted she was ready to give birth. She stayed, and thus began our first battle—her holding on tightly out of fear and me desperate to break free from the confines of her body. It was an intense struggle, a clash of wills, before I even entered the world.

Finally, after 24 hours of struggle, we were both exhausted but relieved to have parted ways. My arrival was met with celebration from the family, and I was a sweet, radiant baby who naturally demanded attention. My father's family welcomed me with open arms, but my mother, unable to express joy, struggled to truly connect with me on an emotional level.

Thankfully, I received abundant love and care from my father, who quickly became the most important person in my life. Playful, kind, and endlessly loving, he was my hero from the very beginning. His attention and devotion forged a deep bond between us that lasted throughout my childhood. However, this strong connection only worsened my already strained relationship with my mother, who grew increasingly jealous of the bond I shared with him.

My Daddy and Me on the Day of My Catholic Confirmation (left); Grandma's Birthday – She Turned 100 on 24.08.1984 (right)

In those early years, much of our time was spent within the embrace of our extended family, both in my mother's and father's hometowns. Interestingly, my mom and dad shared a unique similarity—they were both the youngest of seven siblings.

My mother was preceded by three strong and formidable sisters and brothers, two of whom were lost in the war. Her sisters, with their resilience and determination, managed to navigate life with remarkable success. My mother possessed strength, too, but hers was different. Lacking the courage to fully express it, she channeled it into a different kind of vision—one shaped by her own quiet determination.

When my brother was born two and a half years later, on April 1st, my mother directed all her love and attention toward him—and only him. In her eyes, wasn't he the one destined to bring her the jewels and elegant clothes she had always longed for but never had? This might sound like a harsh judgment of her, but it reflects a truth that shaped not only her life but also the dynamics of our family—especially my brother's.

She was trapped in a deep illusion, one rooted in material desires and unmet dreams, which consumed her inner world. It was her path of suffering, and I bore the heaviest burden of it. I grew up feeling that I must have done something terribly wrong to deserve her coldness and lack of love. She made me feel unworthy, constantly monitoring my actions and undermining me whenever she could. My brother, her favored ally, stood firmly by her side in this dynamic. No matter what I did, I was never good enough.

This is where the foundation of my deepest struggles began—a pattern I carried with me from a much older soul journey. Over time, I came to realize that I had a karmic debt to settle with her, a cosmic balance that required me to endure this challenging relationship. It was a profound realization, one that helped me make sense of the difficulties I faced as a child.

Yet, as hard as my childhood was, it also became a powerful source of transformation. My mother's unrelenting tyranny was a kind of training—one that forged strength and resilience in me. After all, a diamond only forms under immense pressure.

And believe it or not, there were fleeting moments when all the pain seemed to dissolve. In those rare, precious seconds, we recognized each other as souls bound by a timeless connection, meeting again and again to fulfill the trials we had chosen out of boundless love. Those moments of soul recognition were profoundly true and deeply healing, making up for much of the pain. Blessings to her soul. Wherever she is now, I pray she roams free and playful.

Much later, four years to be precise, my little sister came in. She was the most charming little girl ever and got all the attention besides my brother. I receded further into the background as Cinderella, one who is called to do the dirty work and the necessary. My place as the heart of the family, between parents and siblings, was never even acknowledged. I wither into shrinking into myself, into my own inner world, a very mental dream world of imagination and fantasy, a true space cadet, executing what's expected of me, never daring to ask for anything for me but suffering it all deeply within. So henceforth, the image of myself is sourced in bottomless despair and powerlessness, investing all my life force into proving my worth, value and power – and all and all in vain.

And to make it all worse, my parents moved to Hamburg, the place where my father began his brilliant career. I just never got "warm" in that city. It is famous for its long wet winters and strong wet winds blowing, and its cool and snobbish town folk. I suffered in this place from 1956 until 1972.

My sister played out her own game of attracting attention to herself. At the age of 2 and a half, she fell ill, lethally ill, spent months in hospital, attracting one deadly disease after another, ending up perfectly well after all this drama and having found THE method to pulling attention and energy from everyone around her. She, thus, developed a strong dependency on others, and that turned into her downfall: she became an alcoholic at the age of 14. Everyone closed their eyes upon this initially, and by now, she is a ruin of a being on all levels, a being that you want to run from, ugly, sick, weak, retarded, a sorry sight and sound to bear. It has been most challenging for me to accept and forgive her for her choice of living her life.

In my attempt to prove my worth and value by being over-responsible, by leaning far out the window of what is good for me, by losing complete touch with what it is that I want, in fact, and what is the real me, this becomes a pattern. And inside me, I am in an almost permanent depression. Life holds no joy for me, no excitement. Nothing worth living for. I have no permission to be me and live my life.

I am a "born" catholic; my teachers at primary school were "penguins", nuns wearing black/white robes. My parents chased us to church on Sundays and stayed home themselves. We learnt the catechism, yet as I look around me, I see no one abiding by these teachings, and so at the age of 14, I decided to turn my back on this criminal institution called the Roman Catholic Church and its stinking male-dominated hierarchy and quit my membership there.

My father's discredit for the church is obvious. He had been nearly abused by a priest as a child when performing the duties of a mass servant as the boys were expected to do and learning the catechism.

My Little Brother Rüdiger and Me (left)
Illusion of a "Happy" Family... Can You See? (right)

My mother related some insights from my early years to me:

In my first school year, I appeared to have taken the path to school, strolling along leisurely through and deeply enchanted a large, overgrown meadow, which in the summer meant bathing in colours and scents of myriad flowers. I savoured this and eventually picked a lovely bunch of flowers. To share this enjoyment with my teacher, too, I would arrive for class late but with a bunch of flowers and a big happy smile! This happened various times until the teacher reported it.

And at Christmas, I was to recite a poem in front of the assembly of teachers and parents. I started off bravely, but as I went on, my head slowly sank lower and lower onto my chest, and my voice evaporated into a whisper, and all those eyes were on me! The first story related to my true nature, and the second one revealed my broken inner space, where self-esteem cannot grow – bearing ancient trauma.

And when I saw what my parents envisioned for my life, that road that was straight as an arrow and dead on both sides and at the end, I thought of prematurely ending my life around the age of 15. I thought and thought about the possibilities. None of them seemed to taste/feel good to me. One boyfriend who visited me in my home left me for one younger, another one for one stinking rich. What's in this life for me, please? All just negative?

My father shocked the wits out of me one day when he sat reading that huge newspaper, and all of a sudden, he turned one corner of the paper, peeped over at me and suggested I should consider taking the pill. I should what, please? I nearly fell off my seat. And that strange grin on his face! I was not even anywhere near where he was pointing at! Those boyfriends were just friends, nothing was between us. But there were quite a number of interested boys/men around. I was not up for having at all as wrapped up in my inner turmoil as I was then. White-skinned men did not turn me on anyway.

When I was 18/19 years old, one of Dad's friends became like an ally for me. He would listen to my lamento, be there for me, take me out for dinner, buy me clothes, etc. And he initiated me into sex, which was better than a young, inexperienced boy fiddling around with my body. It could be that my Dad was behind this, but I will never know now. And if he was, thank you, Dad. Yet, I remained untouched behind my very tightly locked inner space and ran off.

Radical switch of topic here: My parents did not ever get sick until they got really old, like 80. They both had strong constitutions, which is a valuable heritage. Sickness is not an active program in me.

Whenever we children got ill, they would just apply natural cures and give the healing its due time, that's all. That's how they had grown up and learned to deal with ill health independently—another great value. My siblings deviated from this line.

I never trusted Western medicine, had had enough negative experiences and knew how to take care of and cultivate my health through the power of nature. Since 2004, I have no longer had health insurance.

Dentists are just untrustworthy and greedy for money. That's why my teeth are in an appalling state. But I can eat and smile, still, hahaha, and even laugh out loud!

Three Siblings – Yet So Very Different and Their Parents, Celebrating Something Again...

NAKED

And vulnerable
I enter this world
Lost but for love and care
To sustain and nourish my life
And allow it to thrive.
Life so thirsty for the right grooming
And yet:
It manages a surprising amount of much, much less than that!
Just HOW adaptable it is! HOW far it will bend!
Yet, true life is pure love in abundance, oh yes, it is!
All life craves that pure love
To reach its state of abundance and full blooming,
Yes, it does!
Ei, mankind at present
Lingers in a state of deepest darkness.
Yet life's secret will have it
That just there, in this sorest darkest point
Lies the most powerful of lights
Lies the light of renewal, oh yes, it does!
Aja! So wake up, man, Wake and free yourself!
Feel: your pleasures have long been stale!
Come for the higher taste in life,
I entice you to gently grow
Into your true divine heritage of beauty and noblesse!!!

IsIs 2001 Berlin

Falling out of the Nest

Eventually, after grappling with indecision and a lack of comfortable escape routes, I consciously resolved: Fine, then! Let me live this life completely, right down to the very bottom—every bit of it! Running away never even crossed my mind. Where would I go? I had been so overprotected, trapped in my internal world of thoughts and fantasies, held back and weighed down. It felt like I had been pressing my foot on the brakes for years, unable to lift it.

When I dropped out of high school—an ever-dreary place of "learning"—I left with poor grades even in my so-called "favourite" subjects: Latin, Math, Physics, and Chemistry. Suddenly, I was in the real world, knowing next to nothing about life outside or within myself. What now? I once dreamed of being an air hostess, but my short-sighted eyes disqualified me. Back then, glasses weren't acceptable for that role. My father suggested becoming a secretary at Lufthansa, but the idea left me cold. Eventually, he took me to the Red Cross to volunteer for a year, hoping I'd discover a direction. The options? Hospitals or kindergartens—typical "female professions." I tried both, six months each, and eventually chose kindergarten. It seemed like a way to begin transforming this sick society—or so I imagined back then.

But it was more of the same: boring routines, heartless people, suffocating structures. I felt alien to it all. Was I a robot? University was never an option for me—just more indoctrination into a paradigm I couldn't accept.

Still, I completed my training and began working. At least I had an income. Playing with kids was fun, sure, but the adults seemed intent on ruining their carefree joy, turning it into needless stress. Eventually, I moved out of my parents' house and into a "commune," as was the trend back then—"sex, drugs, and rock 'n' roll." The hippie life.

We dabbled in drugs—just harmless marijuana, mostly for giggles. We experimented with sex, too, though it rarely moved me. Once, I experienced something transcendent: an encounter where we simply touched and explored each other's bodies with our hands for hours. It felt like heaven—pure, intimate, and rare. Heartless sex, on the other hand, was as tasteless as unsalted food.

Commune life, however, was challenging. Sharing a kitchen and bathroom with sloppy housemates meant enduring dishes washed once a week and trash that reeked long before it was emptied. Still, I had my own room—a sparse but private haven. Without my mother's constant demands and control, I had freedom. Yet, unbeknownst to me, my inner patterns of self-restraint persisted, and I continued to suffer silently.

One day, a kindergarten colleague asked if I could host three hippies from South Africa for a night or two. I said yes—I did not know how to say no. A week later, they were still there. During that time, I fell for one of them: Neil, a slim, curly-haired youth with big, dreamy eyes. He was shy and quiet but sweet. Our relationship felt innocent and tender, though I cursed myself for getting involved. They had already planned to tour Europe in their VW bus, and I knew this fleeting romance would end as quickly as it began.

Sure enough, they left, and I was alone, sad, but resigned to my fate. Then, a week later, they returned. Love, it seemed, had a magnetic pull. Along with Neil were his ever-laughing sister Lynn and his talkative, Italian-descended friend Christopher, who could charm his way through life—even selling carbon paper over the phone! Together, we created our own chaotic joy amidst commune life. It was the reckless, shallow fun of misguided youth—alcohol, drugs, and music, all distractions from a deeper spiritual emptiness I couldn't yet articulate.

We travelled to Spain, living a lazy beach life filled with weed, police trouble, and daily spaghetti cooked over an open fire. It was repetitive, a mindless party on a loop. Back in Hamburg, I realized my small income couldn't sustain us all, so we decided to head to South Africa together. Neil and the others left first, and I had to wait three agonizing months for my immigration approval. During that time, my longing for Neil overwhelmed me, and I cried for three days straight, consumed by fears of abandonment. My father, ever patient, tried to console me, but even he couldn't lift me from that pit of sorrow. Eventually, there were no tears left.

My parents were uneasy about my move to South Africa. They didn't understand my decision and worried about what awaited me there. Their concern surprised me, though I now see it as the invisible pull of family ties—a bond I felt more as a karmic chain than a connection of blood. Eventually, the family drama subsided, and the day came when they accompanied me to the airport. With trembling knees and a stomach full of butterflies, I walked through the gate alone, trying to appear composed.

And so, I surrendered to fate, heading to the end of the world to escape that alien place and… and what?

Sweet Young Love

First Escape - South Africa 1972 - 76

I was just 21 when I moved to the other side of the world. South Africa, still gripped by the cruel hands of Apartheid, was a nation divided—humans categorized into higher and lesser beings by arbitrary measures. A grotesque design of human life. What had the world come to?

Upon landing, I visited the hippie market where Neil worked. The ride from the airport left an impression: this land felt immense, sprawling, and open. Broad motorways wound through a landscape dotted with gold mines, their discarded heaps of sand glittering under the warm sun. It was striking—both in sight and scent. Johannesburg, at the time, was a patchwork of lush suburbs sprawled across gentle, rolling hills that stretched endlessly along the horizon. Downtown Hillbrow offered a splash of colour and life at the hippie market—a kaleidoscope of music, art, and a vibrant community. It was fascinating, but I felt like an outsider. My self-consciousness over my stiff, formal English—so obviously a product of school drills—kept me silent, trapped in a negative self-image I should have left behind.

Neil's family welcomed me with open arms. His mother, warm and full of life, exuded an infectious cheerfulness, inspiring me to venture beyond my insecurities. Yet, she often laughed when I tried to speak English, not unkindly, but in a way that stung my pride. Eventually, I came to appreciate her humour, and it taught me to let go of my self-consciousness. I began speaking freely, regardless of how clumsy or refined my words were, realizing that joy lay in connection, not perfection.

South Africa began to work its quiet magic on me. Neil's carefree family embraced me completely, quirks and all. Weekends were spent lounging by the pool, playing ping-pong, smoking weed, chasing ice cream trucks, and taking long, aimless drives in search of more friends. It was a simple, easy life with little to think about and even less to do. At times, it felt boring, almost mind-numbing. But in hindsight, it was exactly what I needed—to let my mind breathe, untangle itself from the worries and fantasies I had cultivated in childhood.

Initially, I resisted the omnipresent weed that seemed to flow through every gathering. Watching others giggle and chatter nonsensically left me unimpressed, my Germanic practicality unable to grasp the appeal. But after half a year, my resolve broke, and I found myself laughing along. Why not?

We explored the beauty of Southern Africa: Swaziland, Mozambique, Zimbabwe, Botswana, and eventually, the breath-taking Cape Town. Each destination was an adventure—lush landscapes, dramatic coastlines, and vibrant cultures. We ventured into the majestic Drakensberg mountains, passed through the tribal Transkei, and discovered pristine beaches along the Indian Ocean. Durban, with its distinct Indian influence, and the Kruger National Park, teeming with wildlife, added to the magic. Some trips were made under the influence of LSD, a hallucinogen that magnified every sensation and deepened my connection to the natural world. While its effects were profound, the physical toll was undeniable—three days to recover from the chemical strain on my body.

To a mind like mine, perpetually on guard, drugs brought an unexpected release. They cracked open my rigidity, cleared mental clutter, and revealed new perspectives. Over time, I understood their role in loosening my neurotic grip on life.

Lastly, I must highlight my encounters with the original peoples of Africa—individuals whose black skin, so elegantly adapted, shields them from the harsh effects of the sun's rays. This experience stirred something deeply ingrained in me, or perhaps it has always been a part of my nature—how could I ever truly know? Observing people has been an intrinsic part of who I am. From a place of inner inquiry, I have always sought to notice and understand details that others might overlook.

I am a keen observer, quietly attuned to the world around me. Without interference or judgment, I sit in stillness, taking in the richness of what unfolds—be it in nature, among animals and plants, or within human interactions. Everything I witness becomes fuel for thought, sparking profound reflections and a sense of energetic resonance within.

Encountering African people left an indelible impression on me. Their ancient wisdom and dignified ways shone through, even amidst the grim shadow of Apartheid. Despite the oppressive circumstances, there was a timeless strength and resilience that radiated from them—an enduring testament to their heritage and spirit.

The downtrodden, abused people left the deepest impression on me. During Apartheid in South Africa, it was common to witness a group of African men laboring under the watchful eye of a single white "boss," who often stood apart, armed with a stick or gun, barking orders in a tone dripping with disdain. Yet, despite the oppressive presence of their overseer, these men worked in unison, their deep, resonant voices rising in harmonious song. They seemed almost oblivious to the white man's shouting, entirely absorbed in their shared act of singworking, blending labor and melody into something transcendent.

What incredible power—to create beauty even in the face of brutality! The sound of their voices, so rich and rhythmic, never failed to stir my heart, breaking it open with a flood of emotion. What a profound strength they possessed: the power of the soul, the wisdom of unity. Against such profound, harmonious oneness, how small and impoverished the solitary armed man appeared. His greed, vast as it seemed, was born of fear—a fear that he alone chose to carry. What a pitiful, fearful fool he was.

Once, I witnessed police forcing a group of African men into a large vehicle using truncheons and violence. After shutting the cage and preparing to take them away for imprisonment, something remarkable happened. Instead of shouting or protesting, the men came together in unity, singing peacefully in a unique and soulful harmony. Their voices carried a strength and resilience that deeply moved me. It was a kind of power I had long sought in Europe—among the elders, church leaders, and those entrusted with moral guidance—but had found in vain. Even within my highly esteemed family, this profound dimension seemed absent. Yet here, it resonated with an unmistakable vitality.

The voices of these men resonated through the air with such fullness and richness that every living, sentient being seemed to quiver in sympathy. The sound was so palpable, so profound, that I felt goosebumps ripple across my skin, cascading through me, inside and out. That deep, earthy resonance, layered with harmonies of a higher order, was unforgettable. Though decades have passed, the memory of that sound still fills my entire being as I recount these moments. It was truly unforgettable—oh, my God!

JIMMY

We occasionally visited a restaurant called "Heidelberg," where an African waiter named Jim worked. He was a warm and kind soul, and we developed a deep fondness for him. Out of this admiration, we often invited him to our home for meals and would ask him to share stories about his life. Jim revealed that he had a wife and two young children, whom he could see only once a year for about ten days. For the remaining 355 days, he toiled tirelessly at the restaurant, serving food to white patrons for a modest income, most of which he sent back to support his family in his distant homeland.

What made Jim exceptional was not just his dedication but also his resilience. Unlike many others in his situation, who sought escape in gambling, drinking thick, home-brewed corn beer, or smoking to numb their harsh reality, Jimmy remained steadfast. He lived in a crowded hostel with countless other men under primitive conditions, yet he refused to let these circumstances define him.

Jim carried himself with quiet dignity, unbroken in spirit. He stood tall and proud, deeply connected to his African heritage—a heritage he honored with every fiber of his being. His eyes, though physically present in the restaurant, often seemed to gaze into the distance, toward his homeland and his people. It was as if his soul resided there, drawing strength from the legacy of his proud and ancient tribal nation—a heritage under threat of being erased by the tides of time.

The impression Jimmy left on me has stayed vivid in my memory, undimmed by the years. He was the first truly human being I encountered in my young life, someone who embodied dignity, resilience, and authenticity. I remain deeply honored to have known him. My heartfelt respect to you, Brother Jim, and my eternal gratitude.

This reflection on Jim also reminds me of Nelson Mandela's autobiography. Mandela endured unimaginable suffering during his 27 years of imprisonment on Robben Island, yet he found the strength to forgive his oppressors and uphold the belief that all humans are brothers. Such extraordinary inner strength and capacity for peace have left an indelible impression on me.

Jacaranda Blooming in Johannesburg

After leaving South Africa and returning to Europe, I made a solemn promise to myself: one day, I would return to this wondrous continent to delve deeper into the spirit of its people and landscapes. What more can I say? Oh yes, to be blessed by the chance to traverse the breath-taking expanse of South

Africa—from north to south, east to west—discovering its boundless beauty at every turn. Nature, such an incredible gift to humanity, surrounds us with her magnificence, yet we foolishly repay her with destruction. Oh, CosMa, have mercy on us, Your children, for we have forgotten You.

I vividly remember our journeys to the north, to Tzaneen, where a river meanders through massive rocks, offering its cool, refreshing waters. There, we could be completely alone, as naked as we were born, immersed in the unspoiled harmony of nature and enveloped by its soothing embrace—healing body and soul alike. The legendary Kruger National Park left an indelible impression on me, a place where humans are merely respectful spectators, confined to the safety of their cars (for the animals' protection), while those majestic creatures roam freely across a vast, untamed wilderness.

How can I forget our first night in the lodge? As the sun began its descent, the moment passed in the blink of an eye—a fiery red orb sinking swiftly behind the foliage. It was a magical spectacle, as the sun relinquished its scorching grip, granting relief to all living beings. A palpable shift unfolded; the sounds of the bush transformed as night spread its dark, velvety blanket over the land. Soon, that very blanket revealed a dazzling canvas of stars, planets, and meteors—a cosmic masterpiece that left me awestruck.

Oh, Spirit, what a magnificent force You must be to weave such profound mysteries into the fabric of existence! My heart overflows with gratitude for these precious gifts You have bestowed upon me. Creation sings Your praises ceaselessly, and I feel a deep, vibrant ecstasy resonating within. You awaken something long dormant in my soul—ah, what joy!

Under the pitch-black, star-studded skies of Africa, I feel my soul come alive. My ears drink in the myriad sounds of the bush, each one a whisper of life's secrets. What a magical night it is! Here, I feel at home. Yes, this is home.

I remember a day when we ventured out on a bush stroll, pleasantly stoned, when the rustling of undergrowth caught our attention. Suddenly, a long, green snake rose before us, its sleek body poised. I was captivated, transfixed by its graceful movements, and instinctively wanted to reach out to it. But before I could act, my companions pulled me back. I couldn't help but feel regret; I only wanted to touch it, to connect with its mysterious beauty.

Reflecting on my time in South Africa, I find myself hesitant to recount many of my experiences with people. Often unpleasant, those interactions seem better left in the past, where the ignorance of humanity is already well-documented. This world carries enough wounds without me revisiting those buried moments. We were all, in one way or another, abusing our bodies and spirits during that time—young, misguided souls exploring life in reckless ways, searching for meaning in all the wrong places. Was it the inevitable fate of youth? Perhaps not universally, but for us, in those tumultuous years, it seemed so.

That era was deeply marked by the injustices of Apartheid. Among the crowd I moved with—mostly hippies and university students—there was an air of rebellion, though often confined to spirited words and lofty ideals. They considered themselves righteous in their opposition, but it was the Africans themselves who ultimately bore the weight of rising up. The vast chasm of injustice between white and black was unbearable. I will never forget visiting a Jewish family's home, a display of staggering wealth and luxury that left me speechless. In stark contrast, the black nanny who worked at the private kindergarten I was employed at lived in a rain-leaking shack, her hard work rewarded with a pittance. Meanwhile, the white memsaab played the role of a grand lady, despite possessing little intelligence or compassion. Such was the sharp divide—everything the white population achieved rested on the backs of black labor. Who, I wonder, was truly more cultured?

As for myself, I drifted from one odd job to another—selling coffee, books at the university, and whatever else came my way. These jobs offered a simple solace, a modest income without the mental toll of greater commitments. Deep down, I harbored an unsettled and insecure inner world, fragile and ill-equipped to face more chaos. Working as a kindergarten teacher had shown me too much negativity—too many founders exploiting their institutions, too many children neglected, too many parents blind to what lay behind appearances. I couldn't endure it anymore.

Drugs and alcohol had a firm grip on us, and we let our lives slip away. In the haze of those years, I betrayed Neil, my loyal companion, by falling into the arms of one of his friends while he was away for work. The regret of that moment still stings. When I confessed to him, I saw the anguish ripple through his body, his pain so palpable that I wanted to punish myself for my selfishness. It created a subtle but enduring rift between us—two frightened children clinging to each other, but now with a shadow between us. Our relationship was quiet and harmonious in its own way, but it lacked vitality.

What I missed most in Neil was his ability to truly talk, to connect deeply. Neil didn't know how to express himself, aside from endlessly singing Bob Dylan songs. While I appreciated the gentle beauty of his presence, his music couldn't satisfy my restless, questioning soul. Often, I couldn't even make out what he was singing in that nasal voice of his! In contrast, the friend I turned to could engage me in long, stimulating conversations, which I craved. I was searching for answers, for something deeper.

Neil, though, was a sweet and gentle man. His quiet kindness was a balm for me, even if it wasn't enough to fill the void I carried inside. I often wonder if he turned to alcohol because of my betrayal. The thought doesn't sit well with me, but life, in its unkind way, ensured I received my fair share of heartbreak later. That's how it goes—sometimes, life's lessons come wrapped in the same pain we inflict on others.

Europe Again

After four long years of carefree wandering to clear my troubled mind, my father finally informed me that I had been accepted into an advanced educational training institution. In April 1976, we left apartheid South Africa, with its escalating struggles for autonomy, human rights, and independence, and returned to Germany. For legal reasons, Neil and I got married, which allowed him to work officially in Germany and enabled me to continue my studies to become a social worker—a career path I was not particularly enthusiastic about.

The only part of the training I truly enjoyed was the arts course, especially the pottery lessons. I loved the tactile experience of shaping thick clay with my hands, molding it without a plan or structure. During one class, we were tasked with sculpting a human head—not modeled after anyone specific, just a generic figure. My creation turned out to be the head of a Black man, strikingly detailed.

A few years later, I had an extraordinary encounter with a man who looked exactly like the clay head I had sculpted. It felt like Kismet was at work once again. Unfortunately, I don't have a photograph of the sculpture to compare, but the memory is vivid enough.

Eat - Eat - Italy

After returning to Hamburg, Neil and I initially lived under my parents' roof. My father, ever thoughtful, had created a cozy space for us, but it didn't last long—for reasons that hardly need explaining. We soon moved into a spacious house in the heart of the city with some friends from my old commune days. Life there was a whirlwind of indulgence: sex, drugs, and rock 'n' roll. Neil was dissatisfied with his job, and I found little joy in my course, so when these friends invited us to join them in Italy to renovate their newly purchased, dilapidated farmhouses, it was easy to say yes.

This couple had once owned a popular pub in Hamburg's trendy scene. Tiring of the grind, they sold it for a good sum, intending to escape to the olive-clad mountains of Liguria in north-western Italy. Their plan was to renovate the farmhouses and start a fresh, idyllic life. However, they brought more than money with them—they were also alcoholics, a fact that became glaringly obvious after we arrived. Instead of working on the renovations, they began squandering their earnings in beachside pubs and restaurants along the Mediterranean.

And so, this indulgent lifestyle became our routine. At first, I was horrified. More of this? But with no clear alternative, I decided to carve out a different kind of life for myself. I befriended local farmers, worked the land they generously lent me, and started a small vegetable garden. The hard labor was grounding, and I loved every minute of it—out in nature, surrounded by kind, down-to-earth people. Together, we harvested grapes, made wine, and exchanged knowledge. Neil and I would ride motorbikes along mountain ridges, gazing at the distant Alps and the shimmering Mediterranean below.

Still, something was off. Our togetherness frayed. Neil grew irritable, resorting to verbal abuse, and the distance between us widened. Foolishly, I thought we could fix it.

Then I discovered I was pregnant. Panic consumed me. Dependent on our financially unstable friends, with a crumbling relationship and an uncertain future, I knew I could not bring a child into this chaos. The decision was clear. Through whispered referrals, I found a woman in Genoa who performed illegal abortions—a desperate act in 1978.

On the appointed day, I arrived at her home, joining a room full of anxious women. One by one, they emerged from the kitchen where the act was done. I was the last to go. The procedure was done on a kitchen table, without anaesthetics. The pain was excruciating, unlike anything I'd ever felt, but I forced myself to stay silent. After what felt like an eternity, it was over. Relief swept over me, followed by exhaustion. Neil and I never spoke of it. He was silent and distant, and I was left to process it alone. Much later, guilt surfaced. I embraced it, sought forgiveness from the soul I'd never meet, and moved forward.

Life in Italy carried on, punctuated by occasional drama. One morning, the carabinieri stormed into our home, machine guns in hand. We all (just us 2 couples) shared one large living cum bedroom together at that time. They suspected our friend of being involved with the Red Army Faction, a terrorist group active in central Europe in the late 1970s. Though they found no evidence, their repeated visits added tension to an already unstable existence. Eventually, Neil and I were ordered to leave Italy unless we could secure jobs—an impossible feat, even for Italian citizens at that time.

So we packed our belongings into an old army truck belonging to a friend and neighbor and headed to Berlin, where we were offered a flat to live in by the same friend and neighbor into whose truck we packed our belongings. In our journey, we had two Indian friends, recovering heroin addicts from a nearby tiny olive village, and a German girl who was a girlfriend to one of them. The men were Sikhs, and one of them was wearing a white turban, which depicted him as such. They were from Tehran and had once been successful architects but fell victim to addiction—a sobering reminder of how many young people sought refuge in substances.

As for me, I drank heavily but always stayed functional, often bearing responsibility for others. On our final trip through Liguria's steep, winding roads, I was the only sober one, guiding our group home despite not knowing how to drive. Responsibility seemed to follow me wherever I went.

During our time in Italy, indulgence knew no bounds. We feasted on pizza and pasta, and once in a while, we would set out on a one-and-a-half-hour trip into the mountains and spend half the night dining in a rural restaurant where all the food was homemade, natural, delicious in taste, supreme in quality and purity and the host was proudly aware of his unique and special gift to his guests. We would arrive around 6 pm and never leave before midnight. Plenty of delightful dishes and country wine were offered and had to be tasted even if there was no more space in the stomach. Dining often turned into gluttony; when our stomachs could hold no more, we'd make room through unspeakable means just to taste more. It was both repulsive and irresistible—a reflection of our excessive, unbalanced lives.

We had our breakfast at Pepito, our favorite café downtown, where we devoured salty bread rolls with savory toppings and pastries filled with rich vanilla cream. Everything in Italy was delicious, abundant, and intoxicating. Yet, excess breeds weariness, and I found myself growing tired of this hollow existence.

Now, as we headed to Berlin, I wondered: Would life there be different? Would we leave behind this cycle of overindulgence and chaos? My garden once lovingly tended, would wither in my absence—a metaphor for so much left undone.

Berlin Berlin Berlin – Geh Mir Aus Dem Sinn!

Oh, how reluctant I feel to delve into this chapter of my life – Berlin! After a leisurely journey in an ancient old van, surrounded by my wonderfully eccentric friends, we took our time, enjoying every moment of the adventure. But inevitably, we arrived in the sprawling city at midnight. For someone like me, coming from a tiny village of just 65 people – most of them already toothless – Berlin was a whole other world.

Wait, hold on. Now that I think about it, we left in that rickety old van, but somehow, we arrived in Berlin on a VW bus. How did that happen? No idea.

We entered the city via the broad West–East thoroughfare known as Bismarckstrasse. From there, you could see the golden Peace Angel gleaming in the heart of Tiergarten Park at midnight. But all I could focus on were the glaring lights, the ceaseless traffic, and the overwhelming noise. It was too much. I screamed, "Turn around! I want to go back! I don't want to be here!" Little did I know then that this city would hold me captive for the next 25 years. S-C-R-E-A-M!

Was it dread? Anticipation? Probably both. Berlin turned out to be a tough teacher, one that would challenge me in more ways than I could have imagined. But what choice did we have? We pressed on, navigating through the city to reach Wedding, a scruffy neighborhood spared the worst of wartime destruction. The old buildings there still stood, though many apartments had no indoor toilets—just communal ones halfway down the stairs. Bathrooms or showers? Forget it. A small basin had to suffice.

And then came the winter of 1979, when temperatures plunged to 20 degrees below zero. The old water systems froze solid, leaving many without running water for days. How did people manage? On top of everything else, the heating system consisted of a cold stove in the kitchen, which doubled as a cooking appliance, and a coal-heated ceramic oven in the living room – cough, cough, cough! Yet, those who had lived through the war knew how to adapt. That harsh winter brought plenty of snow, and they collected it to make do when other resources ran scarce.

Luckily, we didn't have to endure that. A friend of a friend offered us a haven: a tiny attic flat in her villa in Zehlendorf, a posh southern suburb of Berlin. Though cramped, it was comfortable, surrounded by a beautiful garden and tranquil streets. It was a lifesaver.

The partying continued there, but reality soon demanded attention. We needed to earn a living. I found a job – though I won't disclose what it was – and after six weeks, I had saved enough to return to Italy with Neil.

Love of My Life - the Mighty Magnet

Something monumental happened to me in Berlin: I fell in love with an African man from Ghana—BAM! The shock was undeniable when I realized his face was identical to the clay head my hands had sculpted years ago, as if destiny had already carved this path for me. My time with Neil, my previous partner, had run its course. To his credit, Neil handled our separation with remarkable composure—he had emotionally detached long before I did. We marked the end of our chapter together with wine and Bob Dylan's music, parting not as enemies but as friends.

Yet, one moment sticks with me: Neil's bitter remark about the color of my new partner's skin. As a white South African, perhaps it was a blow to his pride to see me now in love with a Black man—the very kind his homeland had once classified with the vile term "kaffir," meaning unbeliever. My response to Neil? Kismet. Fate has its own plans, my friend.

But while my love for this man was deep and magnetic, a heavy conflict churned within me—I didn't want to stay in Berlin. Still, his pull on my heart was undeniable. This love felt like a force of destiny, a pivotal key in my personal evolution. It tethered me to Berlin, even as I longed to return to Italy. For a time, I wavered, torn between two places, until I finally surrendered to life in this city—this city that had once been Hitler's playground.

Why do I mention this? Because in Berlin during that era, you could still feel the weight of its dark history. The scars of war were everywhere—physical ruins in the streets, emotional ruins in the German psyche. Wars are a sickness that ravages every society they touch, whether victor or vanquished. They fracture the natural flow of life, leaving behind endless pain and chaos. Truly, there is never a just cause for such destruction.

May peace prevail. May we, as humans, awaken to the truth that the universe is love—and so are we. It is possible to coexist peacefully, despite differences in appearance, language, religion, gender, or any other misguided notion of separation. There is enough for all of us. Enough of everything.

At 30 years old, I was hungry for something I hadn't even known I lacked: soul food. He, just two years older than me, carried an abundance of wisdom—a maturity far beyond his years. His words nourished a part of me that had been starved for three decades. And in those moments, I knew his love was not just a gift but a necessity for my growth, my healing, and my journey toward understanding myself.

We used to spend countless nights drinking tea, smoking weed, and diving into endless conversations. He talked passionately about politics, the global power struggle, the lies perpetuated by the white man, the exploitation and oppression of Africa, the truths of the ancient world, and Europe as one of the youngest nations. On and on, he drew me into his perspective on the true state of the world. As I listened, I could feel the weight of his words—they resonated deeply within me, vibrating with an undeniable truth that I could not ignore.

Our discussions often veered into the realms of religion and spirituality—belief in God, or perhaps the lack thereof. Through his insights, I came to realize that, at my core, I am not just a believer but a knower of supreme intelligence. I had been calling it "nature," but he helped me see that nature itself is an expression of that higher intelligence.

Night after night, we sat together, unraveling these profound and essential topics. I felt incredibly blessed to share this space and this connection. These conversations awakened something in me, broadening my perspective and transforming how I see the world. I loved him even more for this gift—the way he opened my mind and heart to a greater understanding.

He also shared his knowledge of ancient African ways of life, filled with wisdom and depth. Every word he spoke resonated with me on a level that felt almost spiritual. I am grateful for these moments and the profound shifts they brought to my awareness.

He was a student of economics, brimming with ambition and armed with a plan. A part of that plan required my involvement. One day, he spoke to me about returning to Ghana. I was ready to pack my bags and leave immediately. But that wasn't what he meant. He didn't just want to go back; he wanted to return as "somebody." At the time, I couldn't see the broader picture, blinded by naivety.

He convinced me to help him open a shop selling African food and goods for the African community in Berlin. Completely inexperienced and eager to support him, I agreed. He had already found a location in Kreuzberg, close to the Turkish market and not far from where we lived. The shop was rented in my name, and I took out a loan to finance the inventory. I trusted him, believing he knew what he was doing.

But when the goods arrived, they did not even fill half the shelves. To my shock, instead of taking responsibility, he was furious—blaming me for the oversight. Me? That moment marked the beginning of what would soon feel like hell.

Around the same time, I began to see glimpses of his true character. I discovered he was a polygamist. The first blow came during a weekend visit to a female friend of mine in West Germany. I walked in to find her perched on his lap, laughing and chatting as if I didn't exist. My heart broke. After that, he began spending nights away, coming home in the early hours—drunk, stoned, and dismissive—rolling into bed as though I were just an afterthought. The honeymoon phase was over, and reality was sinking in.

Meanwhile, I was juggling an exhausting job caring for six children from a wealthy family on the other side of town. After work, I went straight to the shop to clean, organize, and sell, only to find him either flirting shamelessly with female customers or out gallivanting. I swallowed my frustration and pain, feeling betrayed, abandoned, and trapped. I had put my name on the lease and taken out the loan, and that sense of responsibility kept me tethered to him.

But things only got worse. He started abusing me physically, coming home drunk and violent. My trust in him was gone. I felt like a ghost in my own life—doing my best, only to be rewarded with cruelty. He openly flirted with other women, brought them into our home, and treated me like a disposable object.

The shop suffered, too. Our constant arguments poisoned the atmosphere, driving customers away. Eventually, he began staying away all weekend, claiming he was visiting a "friend" and sleeping on her couch. After enduring countless lonely weekends, I decided to do the same. One weekend, I visited a blind friend to spend some time away. But even that turned awkward when he misread my intentions and made an advance. Furious and humiliated, I returned home Sunday night, only to face a drunk, enraged husband questioning my whereabouts.

When I told him the truth—that I went to a friend's house and slept on the couch—he snapped. His fists rained down on my head in a frenzy of violence. I screamed for help, but it was 4 a.m., and no one came. I covered my head with a blanket, pleaded with him to stop, but he continued until at last he let go.

The next day, I felt nauseous, dizzy, and weak and called a doctor. He diagnosed me with a severe concussion and urged me to call the police after hearing what had happened. But I refused, overwhelmed by shame and fear. For a week, I was confined to bed, my body battered and my mind spiraling with questions.

Later, I discovered the truth: his "friend" had loaned him an additional 10,000 DM for the shop. She wasn't just a friend; she was now his business partner. The betrayal cut deep, but by then, I was already broken.

Once I recovered, I returned to my shop, only to find her standing behind the counter. I introduced myself, and she immediately declared that he now had to choose between us—her or me. I couldn't help but laugh. I stayed put, working both my job and the shop, but it became increasingly clear that he had abandoned not only the shop but probably me as well. I barely saw him anymore. Eventually, I decided to put an end to this personal hell and sell the shop. Conveniently, he had chosen to travel to Ghana at this time, leaving me to deal with everything on my own.

The shop was sold to a German woman married to a man from Central Africa—at least, that's what I recall. In any case, it didn't matter much. I thought I could finally close that chapter and move on. But life had other plans.

One day, she called me, her voice trembling with tears, to tell me her story about her "honeybaby." He had run off, leaving her with a massive debt she'd taken out as credit. She cried and cried, and at that moment, I decided not to press her for the remaining money she owed me for the shop. She had already paid part of it and taken over the business. I told her I'd shoulder the debt myself—or at least a large portion of it. I helped her sell off the remaining stock and furniture. Though I got rid of the shop, I was left with a significant financial burden to bear.

Of course, by then, I had already ended my personal relationship with my "wise-cracking honeyboy." The last straw had been the way he emotionally beat me down. Each time he appeared in front of me, my knees would wobble with fear, and I realized it wasn't right to fear someone I loved. So, I did what had to be done. I tore my heart out and told him I couldn't be with him anymore.

By that time, we had already physically separated; I had moved into a flat below his in the same building. But when I made it clear that I was done, the real trouble began. Whenever we crossed paths as neighbors, his face would twist with fury, and he would hurl verbal abuse at me. If I needed to discuss anything about dissolving the business, I'd call him instead—but even then, I had to hold the phone far from my ear to avoid damaging my eardrum from his shouting. He simply couldn't accept that I had left him. He told me he had "gotten used" to me and now had to "get unused"—as if that was my responsibility. And then he had the audacity to accuse me of leaving him just to pursue others. Laughable!

Through all the chaos, I couldn't deny what he had once meant to me or how deeply and truly I had loved him. That love, no matter how bruised, will always remain a part of me. Love, I realized, is a mystery—impossible to fully understand even for a rational mind.

As for taking on the burden of that woman's debt, I still don't know what compelled me to do it. Was she genuine? Was it all an act? I'll never know. I only know that I felt for her at that moment and did what I felt was right. After years of struggle, I finally paid off the debt—a hard-earned relief.

This intense chapter of my life unfolded between the winter of 1979 and the summer of 1983—a short yet profoundly dramatic period. Through it all, I became part of a loose-knit African community in Berlin. I found myself drawn to its vibrancy: the rhythm and music, the colorful dresses, the food, the warmth of smiling faces, and the playful, relaxed way of life. It felt wild and free compared to the rigid "civilized" stiffness of white society. I embraced it whole-heartedly—and I loved every bit of it.

Turning to ME

I was now planning my future alone. I had no intention of sharing my home with another man for a while, despite the many interested in me. Instead, I focused on my dream of becoming a healer. I explored various healing practitioner schools in Berlin, believing that this was the right place to start my journey. Eventually, I discovered a beautiful institution that immediately felt like home—the "Centre Path." It radiated a light, joyful, and inspired atmosphere, and I knew right away that this was where I belonged.

So, I enrolled in a wonderful two-year program where I immersed myself in the study of anatomy, physiology, and a wide range of natural therapies and healing modalities—massage, homeopathy, Traditional Chinese Medicine (TCM), yoga, meditation, and much more. My past struggles began to fade, and I thrived in an environment filled with knowledge, growth, and inspiration. The institution hosted seminars led by people from all over the world, thanks to its founder, a Danish woman who had studied under Gurdjieff's school and connected with spiritual seekers across the globe. It was an extraordinary experience.

After enduring so much hardship, I finally found myself in a space of love and freedom. I began to open up—though only a little. I remained tightly guarded, too afraid to lift the lid and confront the despair I carried deep inside. The burden remained, weighing me down. If only I had known how to release it. But what could I do? That was my reality—I wasn't ready to heal.

I remember being asked about our favorite place from childhood. As I reflected, I was surprised by my answer. My favorite spot had been a tiny space under the roof of my grandmother's big house. It was always warm there. The wooden floor had a sweet, homely scent, the slanted roof made it feel cozy, and a small window let in beams of sunlight. It was a place of perfect stillness—no one ever came there. Looking up at the sky through that little window felt heavenly to me. Yes, that was my favorite spot.

Another question was asked: "Where do you see yourself in ten years?" The vision came instantly—I saw myself with a backpack, turning my back to walk far away, alone. How true that vision became!

During this time, I had a remarkable encounter on the Berlin metro (U-Bahn). It felt like love at first sight—BOOM. The woman and I discovered that we were both heading to watch a 4-hour long documentary film about shamans. As we journeyed home together, she invited me to join her at her temple space for an Agni Hotra ceremony the next morning. She spoke of a great saint, Babaji, who had recently left his body in Mahasamadhi. I soon learned more about Him and became deeply drawn to the practices.

I joined their gatherings and found immense joy in the Agni Hotra fires, Aaratis, and dynamic Bhajan chanting. The energy was electrifying! I met others who, like me, were searching, healing, and embracing the experience. In April 1984, I visited the Center of Unity in the Swiss Alps near Brienz—Babaji's largest European ashram, also known as Schweibenalp. The ashram, a grand guesthouse perched atop a mountain, was surrounded by pristine nature. A large Havan sacrificial fire pit had been built there, as Babaji had revived the ancient Vedic practice of sacred fire rituals to purify the Earth's atmosphere.

These cleansing fires were powerful. Mantras echoed as offerings—mainly ghee, clarified butter, and fruit—were poured into the flames. I loved sitting near the fire, letting the resonance of the chants clear my mind while the fragrant smoke wrapped around me. The sound of the crackling flames, the rich aroma of the burning wood, and the sacred energy of the rituals mesmerized me. I could sit there for hours, losing all sense of time.

That first time, I spontaneously shaved my head (mundan). Many others were doing it, and something inside me urged me to join. I had more than shoulder-long hair, and I'll never forget the shock on the faces of my friends, colleagues, and family when they saw me bald! Some were at a loss to understand how I could do such a thing. But I loved it. Seeing my face "naked," free from the decoration of hair, was a liberating experience. Feeling the cold air on my scalp, I wrapped my head in turbans. Even when my hair grew back, I kept it about 1 cm long for a long time, loving the sensation of running my hands over it. It suited me well.

Later, I found myself questioning whether Babaji had truly been the Great Avatar who had resided in the Himalayas for millennia—the root of Paramahansa Yogananda's lineage—or if it was all just an illusion. Conflicted and uncertain, I gradually stopped attending the gatherings.

Around this time, I began visiting the tekke of my friend, Sufi Sheikh Abdullah, in Kreuzberg. I fell in love with the Sufi gatherings—ecstatic nights where men and women came together in a circle, guided by Abdullah's powerful voice and rhythmic drumming. The chants, the movement, the energy—it was a powerful, purifying practice. I was captivated, attending every week for years. Ya Allah!

During the last three months of our training in the Healing Practitioners course, the tranquil, joy-filled spirit of teachers and trainees suddenly shifted into panic—panic over the inevitable test we all had to face. This test, administered by a government-appointed medical doctor, was not designed to assess how we could help people but rather to ensure we would not pose a threat to the public. We were examined on public health regulations, epidemics, infectious diseases, anatomy, and pathology—in short, topics deeply rooted in mainstream medical paradigms and practice.

Suddenly, we were drowning in predominantly Latin terminology, threatening to unhinge my sanity. There were long, almost inexpressible words with ominous undertones—names of diseases, chemical components of hormones, and other bodily substances. No, this was not for me. I stood up before the class and declared, “I’m leaving.” Shock rippled through the room, but I meant it. I packed my books and belongings and set out for Italy. There, I was to look after a vast, ancient former olive mill—now a living space—belonging to my friends, nestled deep in the Ligurian olive mountains where I had lived before.

Alone in that enormous house, I faced the freezing cold. For the first month, I practically lived wrapped around a small oven, feeding it wood just to keep it halfway warm. I unpacked my box of books and attempted to study for the test. By day, I basked in the sun-drenched outdoors, and by night, I huddled by the fire, forcing myself through those dull, uninspiring textbooks. But after a month, I’d had enough.

Then, I stumbled upon the complete works of Carlos Castaneda on one of the shelves. Without hesitation, I repacked my medical books and dove headfirst into Castaneda’s world, studying his work from A to Z and back again. Those books became my bible! Reading them was exhilarating, inspiring, and infinitely more fulfilling.

I had always been an autodidact, pursuing the questions that burned within me in my own way and on my own time. Prescribed education had proven utterly useless to me—I neither needed it nor wanted it.

Soon, even the nights called to me. I wandered alone through the forests, dreamed by the fire, and admired the stars. My life had become beautifully simple—just me and Castaneda, immersed in nature. And then, of course, there were the humorous encounters with the local men. True Italian machos, they had only one thing in mind—amore. Hahaha! Toothless old men, young papagallos—or whatever they’re called—ha ha ha! And thank you, but NOHO! Some even risked life and limb, scrambling down steep slopes on the other side of the river just to sneak a glimpse of me bathing! Such foolishness—too much! Even the allure of Italian food couldn’t tempt me away from my blissful solitude in the wilderness.

After six moons of this heavenly life, my friends returned from Thailand, and I left their house to return to Berlin.

Back in Berlin in 1986, I advertised massage services—only to be swamped by men who could not get their pants off fast enough. Needless to say, they were swiftly directed to put them right back on—because that was not the kind of massage I was offering! Oh, men—what a category of creatures! I became quickly tired of dealing with such nonsense.

Instead, I found refuge in the weekly Sikr sessions at my friend's Sufi tariqa in Kreuzberg. The combination of rhythmic movement and mantras sent me soaring into states of trance and beyond! It was a profound experience of healing and liberation. Afterward, we would sip tea in blissful silence, naturally and spontaneously sharing whatever moved us. Thank you, Abdullah, my brother!

I also rekindled my love for dancing, spending nights lost in the rhythm of discos and dance events until dawn swept me away. I would slip out unnoticed by the trails of admiring men, strolling through the silent, sleeping city back home. Dance became my medicine—it shook off the pain, stress, and frustration of city life. It made me feel strong, at home in my body, and free from the confines of my mind.

I remember having a Moroccan teacher, a Sufi shaman, who led Sikr and the whirling dance of the Dervishes of Konya. I could never get enough of it! Sufism captivated me—the ancient teachings, the communal spirit, the wisdom of the Sufi masters.

During this time, I found myself entangled with four men at once. It shocked me to realize what I was doing—it didn't bring connection, only loneliness and emptiness. Sex, without real connection, felt meaningless. And with my tendency to be overly responsible, even one man was too much. So, one by one, I let go of these unfulfilling pursuits and returned to my own, good-enough self. Aaaahhh, yessss.

As for work, I can barely recall what I did for a living in those days—except for a miserable stint in a government kindergarten. Yes, that's what I did because I hadn't passed the healing practitioner exam (hence the massage ads). Stuck in a profession with no room for growth or change—for either the teachers or the children—I found it mind-numbingly dull, a sheer waste of time and life energy. But at least I had the sense to work only four hours a day instead of eight!

I spent the rest of my time diving into the topics that fascinated me—racism, sexism, the eternal gender debate, history (his story and her story!), God and the world, the why, the how, and the what-for. Libraries became my sanctuary. I devoured books, searching for answers, writing my reflections, and uncovering new questions in the process. My thirst for knowledge was insatiable.

I even brought a dance-theater piece to the stage—The Goddesses Dance Again. I embodied the qualities of the spring, summer, autumn, and winter goddesses, accompanied by two female friends beating the drums to my dance, celebrating the four seasonal aspects of the Goddess.

During my studies, I kept stumbling upon the Yoruba people of West Africa about ancient Egypt, the origins of humankind and so much more I explored.

And then—lo and behold!—in 1987, I knew the time had come to fulfill the promise I had made to myself. It was time to dive into Black Africa, to follow that ancient calling of my soul once more, to return to that beloved continent.

It's Time for Black Africa!

But where to go? Africa is vast—54 countries in total. I spread out my map on the carpet and studied it, letting the names of various countries roll off my tongue to feel their resonance. Intrigued, I looked up some of the countries whose names sounded particularly melodic. Finally, I closed my eyes and let my finger land somewhere—though not entirely at random.

Fate intervened when I discovered an International Percussion Festival taking place at the grand Ethnological Museum in Dahlem, Berlin. Seizing the opportunity, I grabbed my djembe and headed to a workshop led by three Yoruba drummers from Nigeria. They were demonstrating the mesmerizing art of the talking drum. Talking drums? Intrigued, I set my djembe aside and watched, captivated, as they communicated through rhythmic beats—dundun pata pata or something of the sort.

I instantly took a liking to the three men. The festival's grand finale brought all the participating groups together for a spectacular performance in the museum's grand foyer. Seated on the marble floor in the front row, I watched in awe as the three Yoruba men Muraina, Lamidi, and Oje delivered a performance bursting with magic, humor, and breath-taking variety. I was completely drawn in, overwhelmed with joy and enthusiasm.

Now, let me attempt to put into words what I witnessed.

First, their traditional attire was stunning—dignified, elegant, and bursting with color.

The drummers began beating their talking drums, and Oje, the dancer, started moving his feet and body in a traditional Yoruba style, skillfully using his shoulders and hips in perfect harmony with the drum's punctuation. As the rhythm intensified, his feet seemed to fly. Then, in perfect sync with the drumming, he executed three flic-flacs, landed gracefully, and continued dancing. The performance built to a dramatic peak, culminating in three final shoulder shakes that brought the mesmerizing rhythm and dance to a powerful close in honor of Ogun, the god of iron and war. Then, the dancer vanished.

The drums shifted rhythm, and suddenly, a bamboo mat came whirling at high speed, spinning wildly around the stage and occasionally wavering into the audience. It moved with a swift, floating, feetless motion—what fun! And what sheer wonder at who or what was making it move like that! I was completely like a child, dumbstruck, mouth agape in pure awe, my heart flipping with excitement. As the drumming came to an end, the mat weaseled its way back offstage just as mysteriously as it had appeared, its secret remaining unrevealed.

Next, the mat appeared again—this time standing tall. Over its edge, two wooden puppets emerged, one unmistakably carved with female features and the other with male attributes. They began conversing in loud, expressive Yoruba. Though I didn't yet understand the language, I couldn't help but burst into laughter, just as many in the audience did. Soon, their conversation escalated into a lively verbal duel, a tug-of-war of words, all perfectly synchronized with the rhythmic drumming. It was hilarious! By now, people were doubling over with laughter. And so, the eternal battle of genders came to an unresolved finale.

A new tune began. Oje, the dancer, was ready. He spread his arms wide, showcasing the enormous cloth draped around him, revealing its impressive size and intricate ornamental patterns. Once he was sure the audience was captivated, he swiftly gathered the fabric, wrapping it between his legs and over his shoulders. The drums signaled anticipation, building momentum—pa ku pa!—and with a dramatic leap, Oje flipped through the air, landing in an entirely new cloth with a different pattern. The crowd erupted in applause! He repeated this astonishing transformation several times, leaving everyone in awe, wondering how he did it.

After Oje took a break, Lamidi, the lead Bata drummer, stepped forward, his face beaming with a wide smile as the ears of his cappy flapped in rhythm with the wild, pulsing beat. He wore a large drum strapped across his back, its body resting against his front. With one hand, he struck one face of the drum, while the other he hit with a leather strip, producing a sharp, resounding smack. The drum's deep, earthy tones carried a raw power, fitting for fierce male deities like Sango and Ogun, who favor strong, fast rhythms. Lamidi played with all his heart, pouring his energy into every beat. I adored him! He was a radiant force—a sun shining through his drumming!

And here came the dancers—just two of them—hahaha! Both were dressed in Western attire: one as a man in a suit with a ridiculous hat, the other wobbling slightly on high heels, wearing a European woman's dress, a silly handbag dangling from his arm, and a wig. By now, everyone was breathless with laughter—I certainly was! She was a woman, obviously. They moved forward, clinging to each other, their faces hidden behind white masks, even speaking in a muffled tone beneath them. They mimicked the exaggerated displays of affection seen between white lovers, and I was doubled over, clutching my belly—it was too funny!

The man grabbed "her" bottom, only to receive a sharp smack on the hand and some rough words in response. Then, just as quickly, they returned to their exaggerated embrace, dancing stiffly in a comical imitation of how white people moved. I loved it. Then "she" broke away, performing a solo Yoruba-style dance with wild, rhythmic hip movements—flip-flap, left and right, up and down—oh! By the time they were done, I was completely spent from laughing!

When the performance finally ended, I leapt up and threw my arms around Lamidi and Oje in a spontaneous burst of celebration. I soon learned that they ran the Obatala Centre for Creative Arts in Iragbiji, Nigeria. At that very moment, I decided—this was where I had to go! Said and done.

In late November 1987, I boarded a plane from Berlin-Schönefeld (then still in East Berlin), traveling via Sofia, Bulgaria, to Lagos, Nigeria. Before leaving, I dismantled my old life entirely. I quit my job, gave up my apartment, and gave away all my belongings, reducing everything I owned to two bags of clothes and my little Indian Shruti box. Europe—I was leaving!

Many of my African friends from Ghana, The Gambia, Sierra Leone, and Liberia strongly urged me to reconsider. They warned that Nigeria was a land of dark magic, random killings, and rampant piracy at the ports—Lagos harbor and airport being notorious. Wild stories flooded my ears, but none of it mattered. My mind was made up. I was ready to embrace my Nigerian fate. Ha! How thrilling!

I felt protected. From 1983 to 1987, I immersed myself in deep spiritual practices, strengthening my inner self and preparing for this journey. I believed I was following my soul's path, and Nigeria was a destined stop along the way. Adieu, everyone—I had finally arrived in Black Africa!

Into Black Africa at Last

I had my first taste of it as we poured into Sofia Airport, each of us branching off toward our respective destinations. All travelers bound for Lagos gathered in a large hall with a small café/kiosk at the far end and a few oversized chairs that looked comfortable but were made of hard plastic. For a good eight hours, I would have to shift around on one of those.

Even before reaching that part of the journey, passengers to Lagos found themselves crowded in front of a passport checkpoint. More and more Black Africans filed in, much to the openly displayed disgust of the Bulgarian airport staff. But they didn't care. One towering Black man parked his equally massive ghetto blaster on a chair, turned it on, and cranked up the volume. The party was starting! With his shirt collar open, he moved to the rhythm, and I loved it—this was life, this was a celebration, and we had every right to enjoy it wherever we were! The energy was contagious, and those around him joined in, making the long wait for our connecting flight much more bearable. The disapproving stares of the Bulgarian staff did nothing to dampen the mood.

At long last, just as sleep was about to calm me, they announced boarding for our flight to Lagos via Tripoli, Libya. The passengers crammed into the tiny, narrow space of the aircraft. The giant with the ghetto blaster, simply by his nature, occupied one and a half seats and half of the aisle. Every time the stewardess passed by him, she had to squeeze herself tightly along his body, her face contorted in utter disdain as if that would somehow help. I sat back, observing in quiet amusement.

The flight lasted about seven hours, with a short fuel stop in Tripoli. I stepped outside briefly, hoping to take in a breath of Libyan air in the dark of night. Hmmm, Gaddafi's perfume!

Around 5 a.m., we landed at Murtala Muhammed Airport in Lagos, Nigeria—the place I had heard so many eerie stories about. Yet, everything went smoothly. I loaded my luggage onto a trolley and searched for a quiet spot to wait for Muraina, who was picking me up by car. Overtired, overexcited, and now fully alert, I sat down and waited. African timing—if not today, then maybe tomorrow? Or next week?

But after just 20 minutes, there he was—tall, handsome, and polite, a man who had already traveled the world. Dressed casually in vibrant traditional pants and a wide top, he greeted me warmly, and we proceeded to exit the airport.

The moment the automatic doors opened, it hit me—a thick wall of heat smacked me right in the gut, deep into my bowels, triggering an urgent need to relieve myself. Oh my God! Where? How? Now?

Luckily, I found a restroom—grand in its original design but clearly battered by years of use. The stench was overwhelming. I wanted to suppress my need, but nature won. Somehow, I managed under the circumstances.

Now, back to facing that wall of heat again? How would I handle that?

Well, I did. I embraced it, inhaled deeply, and marveled at the rising sun, its soft golden light spreading across the sky.

We crossed a large parking lot where someone offered to exchange money for me, but I declined. We got into the car, stowed the luggage away, and set off—leaving behind the sprawling metropolis of Lagos, then home to 18 million people, the capital of Nigeria's 120 million citizens (now 155 million!).

Ahead lay a three-hour journey north, passing through Ibadan, Ilorin, and finally into Iragbiji. Iragbiji—listen to the softness of its name!

I sat to Muraina's right, with the window rolled all the way down. For all I knew, there might not have been any glass left—it was rarely used there! If I recall correctly, Lagos Airport is north of the city, so we left Lagos behind us surprisingly quickly.

The drive was a perilous slalom, weaving around potholes on this so-called "highway," often forcing us onto the oncoming lane and back again. Yet, Nigerians, shaped by the circumstances of their great country, are natural navigators of such challenges. They have no choice but to adapt, finding practical and ingenious ways to deal with the countless adversities life throws at them. After my initial shock, I noticed the calm ease with which Muraina handled the drive—not as a thrill-seeker, but out of necessity. That realization settled me, and I chose to trust his skill.

As we left the city behind, the open bush stretched out before us, overwhelming my senses. I marveled at the towering Iroko trees, elegant palm trees (oil palms), the velvety plumes of bamboo, the generous banana plants stretching their broad leaves far and wide, the stately pawpaw trees, and the abundantly full mango trees. The scent of the dry land filled the air, mingling with the warmth of the breeze. It all felt strangely familiar—like a homecoming. A deep sense of déjà vu washed over me as if I had known and loved this place in another life.

At one point, we crossed the Niger River and soon found ourselves wading through an ocean of houses—Ibadán—one of the great old cities of the Yoruba people. We passed through Ikirun, a small market town where taxis depart for distant destinations. From there, we drove along a long, straight road until we reached a turnoff onto a dirt path. This path eventually led to Muraina's family compound, where three of his four African wives lived.

As soon as the car entered the compound, a crowd of barefoot children surrounded us, their big, inquisitive eyes gleaming with excitement as they greeted me. Smiling and eager, they took my bags and carried them into the house I was to stay in—Muraina's aunt's home.

Stepping inside, I immediately noticed the chickens. Muraina's aunt raised them, and as I entered my assigned room, I realized it was also home to the young chicks—their "kindergarten," so to speak. A generous double bed stood in the room, complete with a real mattress, but the stench was overwhelming. The floor was an utter mess. I swallowed hard, wondering how on earth I would cope with this. Anyone who knows me knows how particular I am about cleanliness! Orders were quickly given to clean the space, and I gladly left the task to others, following Muraina instead to complete the customary greetings.

As we moved through the compound, the general stench of open sewage struck me—the rivulets of waste running or stagnating in places, the scattered trash everywhere. The sight shocked me momentarily, but then I thought: These people simply discard trash where they live and work. In Europe, we sweep it away, pile it up elsewhere, and hide it from sight. Sometimes, we even push it onto other nations—like the atomic waste dumped in the Atlantic, off Africa's shores. In a way, I found Nigeria's approach more honest. After all, where there is life, there is waste. And that was that. I accepted it as part of life here.

That first night, however, a deep sadness settled over me. I realized, with piercing clarity, that in this country, the weight of human suffering is carried in the wombs, on the backs, and within the souls of women, the strong, strong black women. And yet, I also felt that the patriarchal system was merely a loosely woven cloth draped over the indestructible force of motherhood—the womb power that holds life together, sustains the community and preserves traditions. Even such traditions try to do away with feminine lustfulness in favor of male fecundity – the patriarchal chore motive as a means to compensate for the powerlessness of the male in the face of the feminine.

African Women Say: Well, Women Are Mothers, Men Are Children! That´s It! Naked Truth!

My first night in Iragbiji did not grant me restful sleep despite my exhaustion. For one thing, the gender issue still weighed on me. But as night fully descended and a deep, inky darkness enveloped me in my chicken shack, the African night came alive, and I was captivated by the symphony of sounds emerging around me. Human voices murmured nearby while goats snorted as they defended their resting spots—an occasional chicken cackled in its sleep. In the distance, the rhythmic thump of drums echoed. Then—silence.

Soon, a lively church service erupted, its jubilant rhythms and melodic chants rising and falling through the night, stretching on and on until, at last, it faded into stillness. Silence—so profound it felt almost tangible, expanding into space as my ears reached out for more.

And then, from far away, the deep, rolling rhythm of the Bata drum emerged, beating steadily, nearly touching dawn. Were people performing ancient rituals? I must have slipped into sleep somewhere along the way, only to be jolted awake around 5 a.m. by the piercing call of the muezzin blaring from a megaphone atop the nearest mosque—then another, and another. Their cries, urgent and unwavering, filled the air in a cacophony capable of raising the dead, a call to praise and prayer: Allahu Akbar!

Beyond the mosques, the town was already stirring. Music poured into the sky from various sources, merging into the shared expanse that connected all. Before the sun had even crested the horizon, life was already in motion.

Yet, despite the vibrancy of the day, it is the nights, brimming with voices and sounds, that leave the deepest imprint on me—a time of intimate communion between humanity and the spirit world. The air vibrated with voices lifted in praise, in longing, in a ceaseless exchange of energy. I recall many blissful moments spent bathing in the magic of African nights. Beneath the layered sounds, there is an underlying stillness, a sacred purity that heightens every sensation—suspense, vigilance, presence, depth—surprise. The night speaks of its deep, inherent power, of unseen possibilities, of life in its most mysterious form. In the profound silence between sounds, I felt the presence of the unknown, stalking just beyond reach—the unseen forces of existence, the exhale of life, the whisper of death, the surrender to something greater. It is in that space, in the valley of night, that life is conceived and begins anew.

The African day, in contrast, bursts forth with movement—a polyrhythmic explosion of life. Everywhere, in every corner, there is hustle and bustle, the daily rhythm of individuals serving the community, and the community, in turn, serving them. Life here is communal, shared, and woven into the continuum of generations—clans, families, and tribal nations bound together. Even the dead remain a part of this continuum, their wisdom cultivated and preserved for the living.

A few days after my arrival, I was taken to a nearby Babalawo, an oracle priest. He was a small, delicate man with a lively, beaming face and a mischievous smile. I liked him immediately. After the customary greetings were exchanged and the ritual offering of peace—a kola nut, bitter and medicinal—was presented, he cast his Opele, the diviner's chain, to inquire about me and my purpose among the people of Iragbiji.

The ancestors revealed that this visitor from Europe was one of their own—an ancient soul returning to their midst. They named me Alake—one to be tended to as a precious being. And from that moment on, they did just that.

After only a few nights in the chicken shack, Muraina relocated me to his own compound, into a room he used for receiving visitors. My bed was a simple mat on the floor, and I was given a hand broom made from a sturdy shrub to sweep the earthen ground in my space. From that moment on, this humble room became my home. I was content with the improvement and did not expect any special treatment just because I was Oyinbo—"pepe face"—the charming local term for people of my pale, red-faced complexion. The children even had a song for us: Oyinbo Pepe.

From my new vantage point, I had a clear view of life in a polygamous household. By tradition, the Yoruba practice polygamy—at least, the men do. This means a man is allowed to marry multiple wives, as many as he can support and care for.

In the traditional context, wives and children form a man's workforce, especially on the farm. Family—wives and children—create a tightly woven net of community, where each knot strengthens the whole, ensuring stability for every individual. Procreation guarantees the continuity of life, while rituals preserve ancestral traditions. Yet, there is also an openness to embrace new ways of thinking and living, a willingness to adapt to the inevitable changes time brings to even the most ancient societies.

Shiva was performing His sacred work—casting us into delusion so that we might yearn for liberation and rise to a higher level of existence. Have you ever noticed that "evol-love" is simply "love" reversed?

Evol-love

Polygamy, in its traditional form, requires a man to manage a compound filled with wives and children. Each wife has her own space for herself and her children, but everything takes place within the confines of the compound. The head of the family—the husband and father—must settle disputes among the wives, ensure they adhere to the family's code of honor, and oversee the education of the older children. He makes key life decisions for them, which they are expected to obey as law. Sons must prostrate themselves before their fathers and all elders, lowering their foreheads to the ground in a deep gesture of respect. For females, showing respect requires kneeling on both knees. In this society, respect for elders is an absolute principle.

From my observations, polygamous life is more about the burden of responsibilities and the challenges of managing countless family matters than it is about the supposed privilege of having multiple sexual partners for matrimonial pleasure. The excitement of a new wife lasts only until she conceives—after that, the reality sets in, and what remains is a multi-faceted responsibility.

The children, by the way, belong to the father. When I first learned this, I was shocked and protested loudly. However, after observing daily life for a while, I realized that despite men's authority, a mother inevitably leaves a far greater impact on a child's life than a father. In Yoruba culture, the role of the mother is deeply honored and protected. Sexual relations cease from the moment of conception until the child is weaned, which can be well into the third year. It is believed that semen and breast milk should not mix. This period of physical nurturing establishes the foundation for a child's ability to trust and develop faith in life.

Beyond this stage, a child is considered an independent individual. There is no rigid directive teaching; instead, children grow up within peer groups, where they learn to adapt to society in an organic, almost ingenious way. Socialization primarily occurs within these peer groups, often divided by gender. I find this method of education profoundly superior. Once a child is weaned, their reliance on the mother significantly decreases, and they become part of a larger community of children, where learning happens naturally under the watchful but non-restrictive eyes of all adults. This stands in stark contrast to the Western model of the small, nuclear family, where children are often overprotected and disconnected from communal life. Such isolation fosters dependency and, in some cases, addiction.

Education through peer groups ensures that traditions are upheld in service of the community while still allowing space for the fresh perspectives that youth naturally bring and elders appreciate and honor as a refreshing and lightening impulse.

I recall reading a book about research in an Amazonian tribal nation where people lived in the bush, unclothed. However, mothers carried their babies on their bodies almost 24/7, a practice also customary in traditional African societies. As a result, the child develops a deep sense of trust in life, the Divine, and itself. Is it not introduced to the elements, to all of nature and the community, on the seventh day after birth? From the very beginning, the child learns that it is part of a larger whole—the continuum of the entire family of creation. It experiences a profound sense of connectedness, free from separation, wrapped in love, acceptance, and appreciation. What a blessing!

And yet, such people have been branded as primitive, ignorant, wild, and even dangerous—justifications used by the Church and its missionaries to brutally murder or abuse countless members of these so-called "primitive" nations.

In these traditions, no man would ever dream of interfering in childbirth; it is entirely and exclusively a woman's domain. Women support and serve one another without needing to be asked. It is a service that is unquestioned.

During my time there, I never encountered a child screaming willfully at the top of their lungs. There is no unrest among them. They grow into communal life calmly and naturally. Let me share an experience that illustrates the relationship between a mother and her child:

One afternoon, I sat with a mother and her four-year-old child. The child began demanding something in a nagging tone. The mother, keeping her gaze fixed on the distance, gave no response. The child fell silent for a moment, and then resumed—nje, nje, nje. Still, the mother did not react. This exchange continued all afternoon, with both holding their ground—the mother unyielding in her silence and the child persistent in its demands. Eventually, the mother simply got up and began preparing dinner. That was it.

Interpret it as you will, but to me, this interaction conveyed a clear message: "You are you, and I am I. I do what I do, and that's all." There was no codependency. The child was old enough to accept that the mother had her own needs to attend to.

Children, as soon as they can walk, spend most of their time in peer groups. They grow up surrounded by a vast family, with many mothers and fathers available to meet their needs. In traditional African communities, children belong to everyone; they are watched over and cared for by all, whether family or not.

It is common for children to be sent to specific aunts or uncles for guidance in their transition to adulthood. Sometimes, they go to learn a trade or craft. Additionally, the oracle is often consulted to determine each child's life purpose, ensuring they receive the right support from the very beginning.

Both boys and girls are taught self-sufficiency from an early age. They learn how to harvest crops, make fires, peel and cut giant yams, cook, wash, and even iron their clothes. Many also run small businesses, selling oranges, kola nuts, matches, or other goods from trays balanced expertly on their heads as they walk through the village. In doing so, they earn their own kobos and gain early experience in handling money.

In the family, everyone fulfills their necessary roles. The mother is the heart of the home, cooking for the man (wives take turns) and her youngest children. Meals are often enjoyed in peer groups, with people eating from the same bowl using their hands. Once again, children grow up to be independent at an early age—no clinging to their mother's apron strings!

African cooking and Yoruba fashion are experiences I deeply miss because they are pure medicine—nurturing, satisfying, and soulful. The custom of eating with the hands adds a sensual dimension to the experience, as does the tradition of gathering in a circle and often sharing the same dish. Everyone uses only their right hand to eat, and a bowl of water with soap is passed around to ensure clean hands before and after eating.

Yoruba cuisine comes in two main consistencies: a more or less thick sauce, which is scooped up by a portion of "hand food." This could be pounded yam, gari, or amala—various starchy crops turned into a smooth, thick mash. Each is delicious, but it is the sauce that brings the spice and fresh flavors. All the ingredients are natural farm products—pure, healthy, and nourishing. A staple meal might be black-eyed beans and rice cooked in a single pot, accompanied by dodo (fried plantains dusted with cinnamon, ground cloves, and red pepper). What a feast for breakfast! Or akara, crunchy deep-fried bean balls. Moi moi, a smooth bean pudding steamed in banana leaves, is a delicious snack.

My favorite dish was pounded yam—specifically, the soft town version, as opposed to the farm version, which had hard chunks and a stronger taste—paired with egusi sauce. This spicy, flavorful sauce is made from crushed pumpkin seeds and mixed with leafy greens. Smoked fish was always a treat, its aroma announcing its arrival long before it hit the plate, often sold by street vendors. Nigerians LOVE meat—so much so that if there's none on the plate, they'll ask, "Where is the food?"

I arrived in Nigeria as a vegetarian but gradually adapted, starting with happy farm-raised chicken. Eventually, I even ate antelope, sweet and juicy bush pig, and once, a snake that had unwisely wrapped itself around a bicycle wheel and ended up in my pot. I also tasted the white, spongy core of a palm tree that had fallen in the night. The fat, round larvae inside—having feasted on pure palm nut fat—were fried and, surprisingly, tasted good once I overcame the psychological hurdle of eating worms.

However, one thing I could never bring myself to eat was goat. The preparation process was just too off-putting—after its throat was slit, the carcass was sung over an open flame to remove the stubborn hair. The lingering stench was unbearable, killing my appetite for almost anything. I also refused to eat bush rats, which were treated in the same way.

Generally speaking, Yoruba food is delicious, nourishing, and wholesome. The high consumption of meat is understandable in a society where men work in the fields, trek miles through the bush, and lead physically demanding lives in tight-knit local communities, all within an extended family network that spans thousands of members.

One of the most astonishing aspects of Yoruba culture was how people instinctively knew their exact degree of relatedness by bloodline. Extended family ties were meticulously maintained across Nigeria and even beyond its borders. This has been the case since the so-called first nations of the world decided to divide the African continent into respective colonies of their own liking. They used a ruler to demarcate borders on the map of Africa. Yet, these borders had nothing to do with any tribal territories, just randomly cutting through, disregarding any needs of local nations. Yet, despite these imposed divisions, Yoruba families preserved their ancient traditions and strong connections.

I fear that much has changed since my time in Yorubaland between 1987 and 1996, the year of my seventh and final journey to Nigeria. I feel incredibly blessed to have witnessed such a rich, universal, deeply spiritual, yet profoundly grounded way of life—filled with joy, music, and the simple pleasure of sharing. I was deeply moved by how naturally I was embraced, despite my white skin, without hesitation or reservation. I effortlessly aligned with their ways, blending in as though I had always belonged.

Within three weeks, I had picked up the complex polyrhythms of Yoruba drumming and dance while local youth often struggled for months. For the first six months, I lived with an empty mind—no thoughts, just complete presence in an energetic field where things happen effortlessly without the need for words.

A flood of words poured forth when the elders encountered one another! What a ceremony! The warm clasp of hands, the bowing of heads in mutual respect, the slight bending of knees, and the seamless, rhythmic exchange of greetings—an ebb and flow of gentle singsong rolling back and forth between them. This enchanting ritual was always followed by the obligatory exchange of kola nuts, sacred messengers of peace.

Oh, the radiant glow in those old eyes—eyes that had witnessed and experienced a lifetime of wisdom. The proud, upright posture and dignified grace with which these elders carried themselves, even into advanced old age—often beyond a hundred years—were truly remarkable.

The elders represent a vital pillar of African communal life, serving as the keepers of wisdom and tradition. Yet, this structure exists without formal directives or tangible institutions; respect for elders is so deeply embedded in daily life that it is unquestioned. A son prostrates before his father, touching his forehead to the ground in reverence. Girls kneel as a sign of respect.

African societies are generally organized into peer groups, primarily based on age. Meals are shared within these groups, with men and women eating separately. As a foreigner, I was granted an exception and often ate with the men—an experience that, one day, led to an unforgettable lesson. The food was incredibly delicious but overwhelmingly and unbearably spicy. I relished the taste, but suddenly, my body felt like it was on fire. Instinctively, I leaped up and ran outside in desperate search of cool water to soothe the inferno within me. Finding none, I was taken home to recover, trembling between hot and cold fevers. Eventually, I drank a hot beverage and sank into a deep, healing sleep. That day, I learned my lesson!

My insistence on fully immersing myself in local life—including drinking the same water as everyone else—led to a persistent bout of diarrhea. Unnoticed by me, it slowly but surely melted away any remaining fat reserves in my already slender frame, leaving me reduced to skin and bones. But I hardly noticed. First, there were no mirrors—I was living a bush life, and vanity had no place there. More importantly, my internal state of being was elevated beyond physical concerns. I was constantly in high spirits, surrounded by music, laughter, and an effortless joy in simply being together—celebrating life, free from worries and urgency.

At the Obatala Center of Creative Arts, where I had enrolled to learn the Dundun drums and sacred dances, our days and nights were steeped in ancient rhythms and dusty dances. We lived and breathed the communal spirit, from newborns to elders over a hundred years old. Life flowed naturally—except when my co-wife became jealous of me because our husband spent all his time with me, and the tension was palpable. But instead of heated arguments, the neighbors gathered to restore peace in their own unique way.

It was fascinating to witness: space was given for all to speak, but mediation happened mostly through song and dance—no shouting, no quarrels—just a communal expression of grievances. A small palaver, a few melodies, and soon, the warring parties and mediators quietly dispersed, returning to their daily tasks. The man would promise to divide his time equally between his wives (though to be fair, I had never officially married him). The woman, feeling justice had been restored, would be satisfied—for a while. But I always sensed when Titi's patience ran thin, and I would send Sango to her as a peace offering. But men, do they ever respect a woman's wisdom? Of course not. He waited for the next palaver, and a similar procedure would take place, with the same result and the same consequence.

Ah, human nature! The same is everywhere, yet expressed in different ways.

This intervention—an assembly of neighbors—is a self-regulating community practice that helps maintain the natural balance of forces. It is called upon whenever a matter requires attention. In African homes, there is no concept of private life; the community functions as a living organism that must be actively nurtured. Everyone has a place and a responsibility within it. The natural and effortless way in which this unfolds is truly beautiful! There is no need for police or lawyers.

However, African life also has a shadow side—the abuse of magical power. Magic in Africa and other ancient cultures is not the stage illusion performed by entertainers like David Copperfield. Rather, it was once a science—an understanding of how natural forces interact and how the human mind could manipulate these forces, either for personal gain or for the benefit of the community, such as in healing and peace-making. A dangerous tool in the hands of the wrong people! That's all I will say for now.

I realize now that I have left out much of my personal experience and how my life took shape there. Muraina, who founded the Obatala Center of Creative Arts, was the chief—though I am not entirely sure of what exactly he presided over. Regardless, he was responsible for my well-being as well as my drumming and dance lessons, which had drawn me there in the first place. These began immediately, even though I was the first and, so far, the only guest.

That's when I met Sango, my dance teacher, who had the body of a fairy—slim, light, and graceful like a heron—with a sweet and gentle nature. From the beginning, I spent most of my time with Sango and Muraina, especially in the evenings. We would gather at Labule, Sango's beautiful, self-built octagonal community house, or sit outside, facing the road. At night, the road belonged to the goats, who claimed their space with loud, frequent farting and an obvious disdain for humans.

During those evenings, I often found myself "embedded" between the two men as we enjoyed countless bottles of Stella beer or, even better, the local palm wine. The latter was a powerful remedy against mosquitoes—an excellent excuse to indulge in its heavenly taste. You can drink and drink and drink, feeling nothing but pleasure—until, inevitably, your bladder reaches its limit, and you have to rise in search of relief. Only then would you feel its slightly dizzying effect—whhooopeeezzzzzzoooomm! And then, you would piss like a horse! My God, buckets of liquid will pour out until you find yourself standing in a lake!

Palm wine, rich in yeast, emitted an odor that mosquitoes despised. It was a powerful preventative and dangerously addictive, with a strong, fruity taste. However, it was not always available, as it depended on the palm wine tapper, who had to climb high into a palm tree each morning to collect this precious liquid. Freshly tapped, it tasted like sweet, rich fruit juice. After a day of fermentation, it developed an earthier, yeastier flavor, with only a hint of fruit remaining—a true elixir!

Thanks to my rigorous training in alcohol consumption, I remained unaffected while watching my drinking companions struggle to walk home each night. Their departure was always an amusing spectacle—a zigzagging journey in all directions! Once everyone had left, I was alone with the goats, often stretching out on the wooden bench beside them, savoring the freshness of the night air, the stars above, and my blissful solitude.

It was truly remarkable how seamlessly I blended into this wonderful world around me—a landscape of abundant tropical nature and warm, open-hearted people, both respectful and playful, wise yet humorous. This society, so ancient and well-ordered, appeared content, natural, abundant, and simple. And yet, beneath it all lay something as old as life itself, deeply rooted in existential reality. I resonated with it completely.

Then, I had my first encounter with malaria—the local kind. They took me to the doctor, a jovial young man who already had beer breath at 10 in the morning! Oh well, I thought, what was I in for now? He pulled out a massive syringe and jammed it into my bum. Immediately after, they hooked me under both arms, but despite their support, I still collapsed to the ground. That injection was fit for a horse, not for tender me!

Back home, Grandma, Muraina's mother, gathered some greens, made a fire, and set a pot of water over it. She added the herbs, let them cook, and then made me drink the concoction. It was unbearably bitter, sent shudders through my entire body, and made me sweat as if I were in hell. Soon, my body started steaming out such a foul stench that I was utterly repulsed by myself. In my delirium, I let it all happen without resistance, trusting deeply in the old power lady. I finally slumped onto my mat, and Grandma rolled out hers in front of the door to guard me through the night. I slept like a log and stank like a pig, but the next morning, I woke up feeling refreshed, and after taking a shower, I was back to life once again. That stinky green stuff had done its job well!

The drumming and dancing lessons I took were deeply connected to the expansive pantheon of Yoruba deities embedded in a universal scheme of life. I learned about some of them through the rhythms and dances created to worship them—traditions still actively practised. We spent our days sitting under the thick bush foliage, beating the drums. I had chosen to learn the Dundun drum set, which comprises four drums. First, the Gudugudu, a pot-shaped drum hanging on a long rope around the neck, played with two twisted leather slings. This drum laid the foundation—the ground on which the others built their rhythms. Then came the Iya Ilu, the mother drum, which did the main "talking," followed by two smaller talking drums that played complementary rhythms. I learned to play them all, but I often found myself on the Gudugudu whenever there was an outing with the drums since drumming remained an active traditional profession in those days. I was proudly presented to play for the local king on several occasions. As I mentioned before, each rhythm, song, and dance was tied to a specific deity.

Spending my days with those two friends, I soon realized they were subtly competing for my affection. Well, young and blissful as I felt, I did not rule out the possibility, but I was not eager to choose between them—I liked them both. Unfortunately, polygamy was only a man's right! (Though I wouldn't vouch for the secret liberties women might have taken for themselves!) And honestly, I could not see myself enjoying life with two men. I hesitate to share how I finally made my decision, but one strong factor was that Sango took me to his farm.

Reaching it was not easy. We had to trek for 50 minutes through natural terrain along narrow bush paths. I dreaded that journey each time before we set off, but once we were on our way, I loved it. The trek wound itself up and down through villages, over huge ancient rocks, through forests and rivers! But the real reward awaited at the end—the farm. I could see it from afar, and my heart would leap in jubilation. My paradise! The only "building" was a small round hut with a corrugated iron roof, but the true treasures were the massive rocks scattered across the landscape, offering ample space to sit, rest, and even sleep beneath the shady trees. Oh, how I fell in love with that place! No relentless sounds of town life here—just the mysterious calls of birds and a sacred, heavenly silence.

Approaching the Farm after a Long Trek

The experience on the farm pulled me strongly toward Sango. He and Muraina had been peers almost from birth, often sticking together. Yet, they were very different men. Muraina was a "made man"—a chief and a world traveler with his music and dance troupe, as I first met them in Berlin. He already had five wives, and one day, when he forcefully took my hand and made me feel his penis—boom!—I knew, with absolute certainty, that I never wanted that massive, thick thing anywhere near my sacred inner space. That was the final straw!

Sango, on the other hand, was the firstborn son of a medicine man—a wiry old traditional healer who would rise before dawn, walk his rounds through the bush, and then stick his head into the window of the room I was living in to see what I was doing. He would ask how I was feeling, if I needed anything, if I was happy—an ancient custom of caring for a stranger and ensuring she was comfortable and in good spirits so far from home. Little did he know just how thrilled I was to be far, far away from my so-called "home"!

Tropical Abundance around as Far as the Eye Can See!

Sango was an artist, musician, dancer, and farmer. However, he was not a "made man." Instead, he was simple, humble, kind, and gentle—yet undeniably creative. He aspired to become a "made man," and I sensed that I would play a key role in this journey.

Finally, my decision was made. After my time of learning ended, I spent many cherished moments on the farm. This was the most blissful part of my sojourn in the African bush—roaming freely, barefoot, with only a cloth wrapped around my waist, my body unrestrained and at peace with nature. It was a way of life there; as long as it was in the bush, no one objected.

I would send Sango and his children back to town and remain alone, savoring my solitude. My favorite moments were spent venturing into the surrounding wilderness, exploring leisurely, singing to the snakes as I passed through their territory. My peaceful intentions were clear, and they never once disturbed me. I wandered down to the river, discovering plants and trees, but most of all, I simply reveled in the embrace of Mother Nature—gentle, benevolent, and all-encompassing. What a wonderful gift!

My Favorite Spot – I Often Sleep There

My Farm Bathroom

And I cooked my food on the fire like Titi does here.

Titi Preparing Amala in Her Kitchen

Sango had only one wife, Titi, who was a teacher and a strong, influential woman. We got along well and shared a mutual respect. She had five children with Sango and made it clear that she didn't want any more. She wanted me to marry him and become her junior wife—even though I was older than her—so she could have some level of control over me. However, I neither wanted children nor marriage.

Despite Sango neglecting his duties as her husband, we coexisted peacefully. However, her eldest son, Sunday, subtly resisted my presence. He tried to make me feel inferior and crossed my boundaries a few times until I firmly made it clear that he had no right to do so. He was defending the traditional way of life, but I was not fully part of that tradition—nor did I wish to be. I was there to embrace the experience and reconnect with my ancient past, allowing it to fill and shape me from within.

I became so attuned to the land and way of life that Yoruba words unexpectedly slipped from my mouth, much to my surprise! I felt deeply connected to it all while remaining an individual on my journey to ME/WE/ALL.

Sango's Children Carrying Water for Building

A remarkable aspect of traditional African married life is that couples do not share the same living space within a single house. Instead, each person has their own house and space within the family compound, and children always stay with their mothers. This arrangement allows for an incredible sense of personal freedom in daily life. Each individual pursues their own duties, responsibilities, and pleasures, with men and women often taking distinct approaches. While this experience is universal and tangible, family ties remain deeply respected and nurtured, ensuring the continuity of future generations.

Additionally, the practice of polygamy played a role in reducing the spread of venereal diseases and HIV, unlike the risks associated with having multiple mistresses outside of marriage. Interestingly, it is the first wife who chooses the second wife for her husband. This custom grants her greater freedom—allowing her to focus on her own life, travel, conduct business, and rely on another woman to help care for her children.

I live my life freely, without pressure or restrictions, and people regard me as Alake—the one who must be cared for. I follow local customs just like everyone else, without any special treatment due to my white skin. Here, I am truly part of the collective "we."

Sango often took me to visit an elderly Sonponna priestess. Her shrine was located some distance from where we stayed in Iragbiji. It was a small room within a traditionally built clay hut, with a bare earthen floor—slightly sunken but smooth from the countless feet that had walked upon it. At the center of the hut stood the shrine itself, a large rock of irregular shape, which at times seemed to change form—an enduring mystery.

Each time we arrived, she would greet us by dipping a tiny, well-worn enamel cup into the interior of that "rock," drawing out a foul-smelling liquid made from kola nuts—the revered messenger of peace and health among the Yoruba. Kola nuts were also the only offering she accepted. I drank the liquid each time, and lo and behold, I am still alive! In fact, I could feel its beneficial effects on my inner organs. With its astringent bitterness, kola is a powerful purifier for the liver and offers many other health benefits. Students even chew it to stay awake through long nights of study.

Afterwards, we would sit in silence for a while as she and Sango conversed in the dim, mosquito-filled room. Before we left, she would always insist that I accept a small amount of money—usually 10 or 20 kobos—as a gift. She was a woman of astonishing transformation. At times, she seemed like a young, radiant girl, moving gracefully and full of life. Then, she would appear as an ancient figure, over 100 years old, frail and withdrawn. People would assume her time had come, only for her to return to vibrant life once again—our little, enigmatic priestess.

She continued to heal as a priestess of Sonponna, the god of smallpox, and people sought her help for various ailments. However, I never delved into her secrets; they remain well-guarded to this day.

And yet, some of these mysteries were unveiled to an outsider—Susanne Wenger, an Austrian artist who chose to live among the Yoruba in Oshogbo, the neighboring town. There, she became the guardian of the grand Oshun shrine, which has existed since time immemorial. After moving to Oshogbo in the 1950s, she was initiated into the priesthood of Oshun, the river goddess. Wenger physically defended the shrine, ensuring its survival. Today, it remains a sacred site, adorned with numerous clay deities, spirits, and other figures she created. Thousands of pilgrims from the Americas, worshippers of Oshun, and many locals continue to visit this revered place.

Assembly of Gods and Nature Spirits along the Road to the Oshun Shrine in Oshogbo

I cannot resist showing you this image of a contemporary Yoruba goddess—radiating modern style in traditional garb! Woman power!

There was so much more to share, yet my blissful time in Nigeria eventually came to an end. My visa expired, the rainy season signaled its arrival, and I had to return to the land of the white man. Had I chosen to officially marry my Nigerian Yoruba man, I could have stayed there forever. But giving up my personal freedom and binding myself to a man again? Even if that man was a kind, loving, and simple soul—yet an alcoholic? In the end, I had no choice but to leave after that incredible first half-year. It was dreadful! I didn't want to go. I cried crocodile tears all the way on the plane, and seeing all those Oyinbo Pepe faces again in Sofia, I felt their disconnection and was truly in despair. But what could I do? Kismet, once again!

Back to Berlin It Is! Malaria with Me

I still had bank debts to pay—sh...!

Malaria Tropica had me in its grip. Unaware of this, I drifted deeper and deeper into delirium until, at the last moment, I was carried on a chair into an ambulance and rushed to the hospital. The doctors started working on me immediately, though I was already on my way out. What heavenly peace I experienced! I traveled through a tunnel of white light, savoring the sensation of freedom from my physical body.

Someone slapped me across the face a couple of times and asked my name. For my life, I neither cared nor could I remember. Instead, I slipped back into that silent, peaceful expanse. Again, they dragged me back—harshly. This battle went on for a while until, at last, the decision was made: I was staying. Grump!

What a beautiful, blissful journey that had been gifted to me! Dying is, indeed, peaceful. You simply slip away into another realm, inviting exploration. But it wasn't my time—what a pity.

My blood had been almost completely replenished, and a substantial amount of quinine was pumped into my body to help me conquer the multitude of malaria parasites that had invaded me so stealthily.

I vividly recall how this uninvited visitor found me: Sango and I had spent a week on a beach near Lagos, sleeping in the sand. It was fine—until one night. A thick, humid heat spread through the air, bringing with it myriads of mosquitoes from God-knows-where. I remember running along the shore, trying to fight them off, but the more I resisted, the more they swarmed. The battle was utterly futile. Exhausted, I collapsed onto the sand, surrendering. I was covered in bites, drenched in sweat, and utterly exposed. That's when I received my full dose of Malaria Tropica.

At first, it shakes you violently—waves of heat and cold alternating until your bed rattles. I suffered splitting headaches. But then, gradually, all of it fades into delirium. A space of detachment opens, carrying you—mmmmmh. A feeling of weightlessness spreads. Light. Void. It was a profound experience, a gift from Malaria Tropica itself—the experience of dying. And now I know: I need not fear death. That is a precious gift. Thank you!

The young doctor in charge seemed to take a particular interest in me. Once I had returned to the land of the living, he frequently sat by my bedside, feeding me warnings about the dangers of Africa—the lurking diseases, the risks of living among "primitive" peoples. I quickly shut him down. When he suggested an HIV test, my patience snapped. A torrent of angry words tumbled out. Finally, he backed off—fool that he was! They claimed HIV originated from West African monkeys, creatures defenceless against such unfounded accusations. Meanwhile, these same white men had manufactured it in their laboratories as a weapon against natural folk. Groooowwwllll!

My parents flew in from Hamburg. My mother ran to my bedside and embraced me with so much love—I was stunned! My father, on the other hand, shouted. Was I insane? It was his way of expressing worry, shock, and, perhaps, attachment—if not love.

They took me home to Hamburg and pampered me, trying to put some meat back on my bones—I had become a walking skeleton! It was shocking. They issued stern warnings, but they went in one ear and out the other. As soon as I was strong enough, I boarded a plane once more—back into the bush of Black Africa.

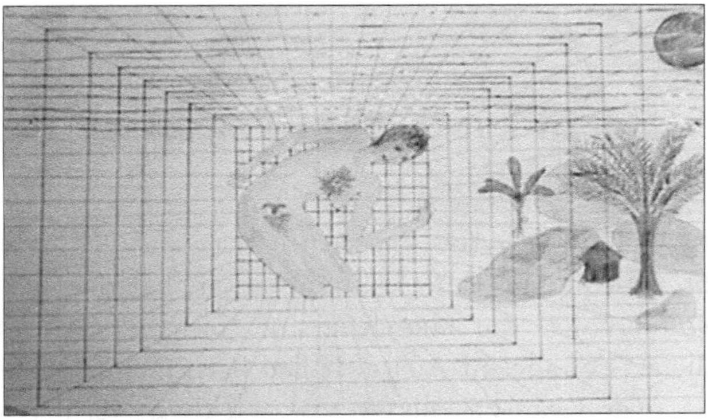

This Is How I Felt Back in White-Man-Country

And So, in Late 1988, I Was Back Again

This time, however, the experience was entirely different. I brought with me a wealth of information that deeply inspired me—Nommology, the knowledge of Nommo, rooted in the symbolic arts of ancient Africa. It had been meticulously pieced together over years of solitary research by a German woman, Gisela von Frankenberg (1925–1985), and showcased in a 1975 Munich exhibition titled 25,000 Years of Knowledge as Art.

She asserted that the artwork of an African American artist, Larry Compton Kolawole, depicted a universal primal alphabet. Through extensive research, she gathered symbols from ancient cultures worldwide and discovered striking similarities among them, leading her to conclude the existence of a universal alphabet. Building upon this, she formulated a world theory based on these symbols.

For me, finding this vast body of knowledge was a turning point. It validated years of my own research into the truth of African culture and confirmed my intuition about the ancient origins of wisdom, expressed through abstract symbolism. This wisdom manifested in various creative forms—rhythm and music, dance and poetry, song and oral tradition, and even the art of divination. All of it carried cosmic vibrations, expressed directly through human creativity. It was Africa's invaluable contribution to humanity's spiritual heritage—one that the West has blindly denied and trampled in its relentless pursuit of material wealth and intellectual reductionism.

Naturally, I wanted to share this with Sango, given his background as a Yoruba artist. Yet, every time I tried to discuss it with him, he would fall asleep within moments. Was it too much mental input? I never found out, but his lack of engagement frustrated me—I was burning with excitement, yet he remained unmoved.

Fueled by this passion, I put my thoughts into writing and crafted a stage play chronicling 25,000 years of human history—and herstory. I was determined to set the record straight, to bring to light the truth about the ancients, particularly those of Africa. There I was, in the heart of the African bush, seeking to revive its cultures and peoples from the false narrative of being "primitive." The correct term, I realized, was primal—original, primeval, foundational.

The Yoruba, for instance, possessed a complete cosmology—profound cosmic principles governing life, the universe, and humanity's role within it. Their society had been masterfully structured, a testament to wisdom and order. Adunni, the Austrian Oshun priestess, shared with me her experiences with deeply spiritual individuals she had known in her early years in Oshogbo. Yet, even back then, she noted, a decline in spiritual strength was already perceptible.

I had a glimpse and taste of the spiritual strength of the Yoruba when Sango took me to the town of Ile Ife, which means "City of Love"—the heart of traditional Yoruba culture - and to the old palace. As we arrived, a group of men in the prime of their lives stood assembled outside the palace, their presence immediately captivating me with its power and energy. Tall and strongly built, their heads shaven, they wore plain white cloths wrapped around their waists and draped over their shoulders. They exuded an impressive inner strength.

Respectfully, we approached them, hoping for the possibility of being shown around the palace and its compound. We were warmly welcomed, greeted extensively in the traditional manner, and then guided through the premises by one of the men. Along the way, I listened to mind-boggling stories tied to various sacred spots. Let me attempt to recall them.

I remember a well so deep that one could not see the surface of its watery depths—naturally, a mysterious story accompanied it. Then there was the fire pit of the first smith, Ogun. Our guide recounted the Yoruba story of the world's creation, according to ancient lore. This was over 30 years ago, so forgive me if I cannot recall all those mysterious places of creation. They left a lasting impression on me, filling me with both wonder and skepticism—my mind wrestling with the supernatural and the rational.

While in Ile Ife, I stumbled upon a blacksmith's workshop—an open enclosure with a short clay wall, allowing me to watch the smith at work on the bellows. I observed him for a while, utterly fascinated. It was such a primal, almost sacred act. I could feel the weight of this ancient profession, which held a deep significance within the Yoruba spiritual tradition.

The Yoruba are undoubtedly one of the most prominent ancient civilizations. Their spiritual tradition (I hesitate to use the word "religion" here, as it has been tainted by the historical misuse of power by the Abrahamic faiths and their political institutions) has endured across the Atlantic, where, against all odds, millions in the Americas continue to practice it—albeit in slightly altered forms—to this day. They are a proud people, deeply rooted in their rich, wise, and ancient heritage—one based entirely on existential reality. Despite the infiltration of Western ideologies, the influence of Christian sects, and the growing fundamentalism of Islam, they have held steadfast to their traditions. And let me tell you—their traditions are incredibly rich and powerful in every conceivable way. They have every reason to be proud!

Yet, I would probably be shocked by the transformation Nigeria has undergone in the past 20 years since I was last there. It is a nation blessed—perhaps even burdened?—with vast mineral wealth, but even more significant is its boundless human resourcefulness and creative power.

I must also speak of Nigeria's legendary hero: Fela Anikulapo Kuti—musician, revolutionary, mystic, and insatiable polygamist—who once arrived in Berlin for a concert with his newly married 22 wives! He was small and lean, yet his voice, message, and presence were larger than life. I had the chance to visit his Lagos shrine on a Friday night, eagerly awaiting his performance. It was a long wait. The air grew thick with marijuana smoke, the haze enveloping the hall as the anticipation built. Finally, at 2 a.m., he appeared—his sax slung across his shoulder, a massive joint in hand. And then the party erupted!

What a beat! A hypnotic fusion of jazz, Yoruba traditional rhythms, and his unmistakable style of socially critical music. The hall pulsed with energy—feet itching to dance, bodies moving in unison. This hero, however, would later succumb to HIV, his tragic demise serving to raise awareness of the epidemic. His funeral was a grand procession through Lagos, a city brought to a standstill as thousands joined in celebrating his extraordinary life. What a mighty being he had been!

The Little Farm Hut

Back to Nommology, Iragbiji and Sango

My mind grew creative. I began envisioning a spiritual artist's village on Sango's land, surrounding the farm. We spun the idea together, refining it until it became more and more concrete in our minds. Sango wasted no time—he was already clearing more farmland to provide for future visitors from all over the world.

The next step was a well. Hausa men from the north arrived to dig it—a deep hole about two meters in diameter. I watched them labor under the scorching heat for days, sweat pouring down their backs as they worked tirelessly. Massive amounts of rich, fatty soil were excavated and repurposed to create sun-dried bricks for the well's walls and the first round hut, which had a diameter of about eight meters.

The mud—mixed with straw, sand, and water—was prepared by stomping it with our bare feet, an oddly satisfying process. Once the mixture was ready, we dug a shallow trench to mark the hut's circumference. Then, grabbing as much mud as we could hold, we began slamming it onto the ground to form the base of the hut's walls. Layer by layer, we built up the structure, leaving an opening for the entrance. After reaching a height of about 25 to 30 centimeters, we let it dry for a few days before adding the next layer. This process continued until, finally, we reached head level. Small openings were left for windows.

There were many idle days forced upon us as we had to wait patiently for the walls to dry. At last, the roof was due. It would be a palm-frond roof. A simple support structure was built, onto which the palm leaves were mounted and secured—DONE! This called for a celebration!

The children eagerly harvested yams and vegetables, while Sango, ever the skilled hunter, went in search of bush meat, which he greatly enjoyed. A fire was made, and a massive pot was set atop it, filled with water. Yams were peeled and chopped into pieces, ready for the next stage. The large, heavy wooden mortar was thoroughly cleaned, and the equally weighty pestle was prepared—pounded yam was on the menu.

Feeling enthusiastic, I decided to take over the pestle, eager to contribute. To my utter dismay, I could barely lift the thing, let alone pound yams with it! What kind of unearthly strength did these people possess—children included? I soon learned that pounding yam was traditionally a woman's task and not a solitary one—several women worked together in perfect rhythm.

Pounding yam, I discovered, was an art in itself—and an exhausting one at that! It took immense effort and buckets of sweat. But what a spectacle it was! The rhythmic pounding, the pestles flying up and down in synchronized motion, the pieces of yam slowly transforming into a smooth, thick mash. Sweat dripped, backs bent, arms lifted—it was mesmerizing. These women possessed an invincible strength!

During the process, solid bits had to be removed to achieve the perfect, silky texture.

There was usually a specific order to who ate with whom, but on that day, we all ate together—sitting on the ground under the shade of the trees, savoring the fruits of our labor: the beautiful hut we had built and the generous bounty of the bush that had sheltered and nourished us so lavishly. Eating in the bush was a joy. Any overlooked solid pieces of yam could be flicked away, and the bones from our meal were casually discarded behind us, left for whichever creatures might relish them. Whatever remained was offered to the bush animals and spirits. Even the dishes were washed just before eating, ensuring that they, too, had their share. The continuum of life was everywhere.

We were thrilled to have completed the well and our first round hut. And while we were at it, Sango had also created a small space for me to shower—a circle of palm leaves stuck in the ground, their tips bound together, forming an enclosure just big enough for me and my bucket, shielding me from prying eyes as I took my bush shower. What a luxury! Even our most basic needs were seamlessly woven into the land's natural rhythms. Any "pipicaca" business, as we called it, was directly contributed to the fertility of the bush.

I found myself growing ever deeper into alignment with this simple, natural way of living—above all, it was free! I loved it. I thrived on it. I remember one full-moon night in Iragbiji, during Labule, when people gathered to drink, chat, and play music. On a whim, I picked up the big Bàtá Iya Ilù—the mother drum—sat myself down, placed it over my legs, and started to play. Pa ku pa, pa ku pa—slowly at first, but then, as if possessed, I gained speed, striking the drum with effortless precision as though it had been my daily bread. People glanced at me and nodded knowingly: "Aah, the spirit of the drum has entered her." And on and on I went, effortlessly replaying rhythms I had absorbed for months. It had become a part of me.

What a joy it was! I can only compare it to riding a horse—when rider and horse become one, flying together in perfect harmony. That night, I felt the same connection with the drum. It carried me, lifted me, played through me. The spirit had taken hold, and I surrendered to it—freedom!

That was special. In truth, I was deeply attuned to this life, embraced by a benevolent and powerful community. In return, I was immersed in nature's abundant beauty beneath the vast cosmic roof that stretched above me, night after night. What bliss! Aaaahh, gratitude!

But back to reality. I felt limitations in my relationship with Sango. Sexually, I was constantly frustrated. Mentally, we were mismatched. He was gentle and kind, and he had a genuine interest in our collaboration. But beyond that?

It was time to return to Europe. Six moons had passed once again. 1989.

This time, I found myself pregnant. And it was clear—I did not want Sango's child. In fact, I did not want a child in my life at all. I was not ready for such an immense responsibility, nor did I want to be bound to him forever. So, I sat in meditation, connected with the soul, and explained why I needed to send it back. I asked for forgiveness and offered my blessings. I felt a response—an acceptance from within—and something shifted inside my belly.

Next, I had to face the procedure. Since I was already in an advanced stage, nearing the end of the third month, the only way to proceed was to feign psychological instability. I was interviewed, spoke bluntly and plainly, and passed. The abortion was approved. It would be like giving birth.

At the hospital, I was given a single room, and the process was artificially induced by injection. I hated every moment of it. Hours passed with no sign of labor, yet every hour, a different doctor came in, coldly inserting their fingers into my sacred space—without so much as looking at me, let alone speaking to me. Heartless. Mindless.

Finally, after twelve hours, a searing pain tore through my lower belly—aaahh—it was time. The so-called professionals told me to lie down, but I refused. How foolish to give birth lying down—only men can come up with such nonsense. I sent them all out and did what needed to be done. I breathed as if my life depended on it—because it did. I knelt on the bed, braced my hands on my thighs, and pushed my belly down. It was hard work—gods, it was hard! But at last, finally, the birth canal opened, and in due time, a tiny, doll-like form emerged.

It was stiff. It had been dead for a while. And its skin was pitch black.

The nurse tossed it into a trash can—clack.

How fragile life is. And yet—it is an illusion.

Society, religion, the Church—they make women feel guilty for rejecting what they call a "gift from God." But I felt no guilt. Not then. That came later when I began to reflect on forgiveness. I had to forgive myself first—for getting into this situation, for not paying closer attention. But in the end, I understood—there was no reason for guilt. Shit happens.

That is why I can write about it now, openly, without shame. More than anything, I want to inspire all to create a world where welcoming new life is a joy—where women are safe, honored, supported, and acknowledged in their sacred role as life-bearers, teachers, and guides for future generations. We must dismantle out-dated taboos, rigid moral standards, and the blind denial of nature itself. This is the core issue of human society. The gender issue.

It is crying out for correction, healing, truth, balance, collaboration, understanding, and complementarity. And most of all—for a return to real communal living.

But for now—the ordeal was over. And I felt strong.

And guess what?

Right. It was time to return once again.

A week before the Berlin Wall—built to divide East and West Germany into two different nations—finally fell, I boarded a plane back to Lagos, Nigeria, in November 1989.

This time, I knew my time with Sango in Iragbiji had come to an end. I found a place to live in Oshogbo, the next larger town, world-famous for its Osun shrine and for Adunni, aka Susanne Wenger—the Austrian artist who moved to Oshogbo, settled there, and was initiated into priesthood around 1950. I mentioned her before.

Oshogbo Plus

A Detail of One of Her Works

Another Creation of Hers, So Blending into Nature

I visited her many times. This powerful woman was highly respected and revered by many of her Yoruba contemporaries—feared by others. Her home was unmistakably that of an artist, with a beautifully carved fence enclosing her front terrace, a richly adorned wooden door, and thick foliage from creeping plants covering nearly the entire front of her towering two—or possibly three-story house.

We had many conversations—or rather, she answered countless questions of mine about Yoruba lives, the Yoruba gods, and their ways of understanding the world, the cosmos, and the divine. She spoke of humanity's role in this grand scheme we call life. Much of it has since faded into the depths of my memory, but the essence remains: an inspiring, open, and all-embracing worldview—one that, like those of ancient peoples across the globe, saw the universe not as something to be conquered, but as something to be in harmony with.

Yes, and it deeply resonated with my soul. The physical world is merely a reflection of our inner space—its contents, ideas, concepts, and consciousness. She was an extraordinary being, living among birds, chickens, snakes, and monkeys in her home. Many locals considered her eccentric and even feared her. Yet, at the same time, she was a mother to many Yoruba children, guiding them through their deep and rich spiritual heritage by example. She taught them how to create cultic art, for which she had become renowned. She welcomed them into her home, and together, they shared a traditional way of life.

Over time, she became highly respected among the Yoruba people, and she was honored with prestigious traditional titles and responsibilities. She had become an inseparable part of this ancient and wondrous way of life. Blessings upon her soul!

I spent my 40th birthday in December 1989 at the Oshun shrine, directly on the banks of the river, in the shade of that towering sculpture called Iya Ma'apo.

Iya Maa'Po, the Great Mother Goddess

Sitting in that place of power, my ears buzzed with the sound of a trillion insects, their hum penetrating my mind and lulling me into a trance-like state. I remained there all day, lost in deep meditation—one with EarthMa and the sculpture, which seemed to have risen naturally from the earth itself, a powerful mother goddess—one of Adunni's magnificent creations.

I asked her to initiate me, but she refused, saying it was not my path. Still, she left an indelible mark on me—an entirely independent, extraordinary, and powerful woman who had followed her calling with unwavering dedication. She was a wise spiritual guide to many across the globe. My deepest reverence!

She had protected the Oshun shrine against worldly interests with her own body. The sites she created have since become part of humanity's shared heritage. She left behind an incredible legacy before departing this world at the age of 94 in December 2009.

I must share how I first came across her story! In my teenage years, my parents received the Stern magazine regularly. One particular edition featured Adunni's extraordinary story, accompanied by stunning photographs. Can you imagine my reaction when I discovered that article? I tore the pages from the magazine and kept them for years, dreaming that one day I would meet this remarkable woman.

Over time, the memory of that article faded. When the opportunity arose to explore Africa's diverse cultures and traditions, I had long since lost those treasured pages—most likely discarded unknowingly. Yet, the power of manifestation worked its magic.

In Oshogbo, a city renowned for its artists, I met many so-called creatives. However, few were as deeply rooted in ancient spiritual traditions as she had been.

Now, I shift back and forth between Iragbiji and Oshogbo, making the transition gradually to soften the pain for Sango, who had hoped we would realize our dream of building a spiritual artist village on his farm. Bit by bit, I carry my belongings back. I am slowly returning to myself, no longer immersed in that wonderful communal life.

That period was a vulnerable time for me. Men pursued me, and in a way, I was "on the market," seeking a companion who aligned with me on every level. It was a confusing phase, and I made the mistake of falling for someone completely unworthy. Forgiving myself for that took time—I had been such a fool! Oh my God!

During that time, I met many fascinating people, some of whom had been exposed to Western influences. While this allowed for common ground, it also introduced corrupted ways of thinking that often led nowhere. Yet, amidst the confusion, I encountered one truly remarkable man. He was a well-known and sought-after astrologer—a true light being.

On multiple occasions, he restored my energy simply by holding my hands on his own, grounding me, and guiding me back to myself. His name was K.K. Yope. Around 50 years old, he had a wife and two lovely daughters. He was a pure soul who asked for nothing in return. In those days, he was my saving grace.

Tragically, out of nowhere, he fell victim to a sinister magical practice. At the peak of his life and career, he suddenly collapsed—gone, just like that. Black magic is one of Nigeria's darker realities, and this is why my African friends had always warned me against venturing there. I survived, but K.K. did not. Blessed be his beautiful soul!

Oshogbo is home to many traditional Yoruba artists who create magnificent works using a variety of materials. One of the most authentic forms is indigo batik, used in traditional clothing and large, intricate wall hangings that depict stories of gods and ancestors. These pieces, woven with mesmerizing colour compositions, preserve ancient lore.

There is no limit to the creativity of these artists. They use an astonishing range of materials to express the essence of Yoruba tradition. Art, at its core, originates from the sacred—it was once deeply intertwined with spiritual worship. When its primary purpose shifts from sacred expression to mere commercialism, it gradually loses its transformative power for both the artists and the observers. Artifacts hold meaning and energy as long as they serve their intended purpose. Once reduced to mere decoration or a means of survival, their spiritual potency fades.

This is how the old worlds are systematically corrupted: poverty is imposed, desires are artificially created, and then those affected are labeled as incompetent, primitive, or ignorant. This, in turn, justifies further cultural and economic exploitation. Resources are plundered, traditions are stolen, and markets are flooded with inferior goods. Glorious white nations—what have you imposed on this planet? Are you merely Shiva's tool, leading the world from delusion to liberation?

The white nations were able to do what they did because they found allies among the very people they colonized, "Christianized," exploited, robbed, and suppressed. The Yoruba princes were sold to slave traders by their own kinsmen and shipped to America. The truth must be told. Human weakness, ignorance, greed, and hatred have always been part of history, but they are being addressed now more than ever.

I traveled extensively and visited Ile Ife, where I had friends on the university campus. We would sit together, talk, and party. It was an interesting glimpse into their way of life—fascinating yet not entirely fulfilling.

Unilag, the University of Lagos, was another stop in my exploration of Nigeria. There, I met many young students and was introduced to professors deeply immersed in Yoruba traditions—remarkable individuals with profound knowledge. Many engaging discussions took place, though most remained on the surface. The most rewarding moments were spent sitting by the lagoon, watching fishermen at work, observing the birds doing the same, and soaking in the peaceful beauty of nature. The towering trees and the park-like campus added to the serenity.

Victoria Island was another place I explored, though with some distaste. Here, the extremely wealthy live behind high walls topped with barbed wire, consumed by their work and their own dramas. Most embassies are located in this area as well, adding to its eerie atmosphere. The contrast between Victoria Island and other parts of Lagos is staggering. In some areas, people live in such inhumane conditions that it is almost unimaginable. I once walked through one such place—the stench of sewage was nearly visible, and there was little to indicate human habitation. Cardboard boxes, trash, and rubble stretched as far as the eye could see.

And yet, the people living there had made a choice. They had left their ancestral lands, their structured village life, and their sense of communal security in pursuit of fortune and a so-called "better" life in Lagos—the massive, chaotic metropolis that swallows dreams and spits out despair. The government even offered financial incentives for them to return home, but the illusion of wealth, fueled by television, had taken root in their minds. And so, they endured conditions unworthy of human existence, clinging to the dream of one day making it big. They bore every hardship imaginable, driven by relentless hope. What has become of the human race?

Perhaps the most remarkable thing about my travels was that I was never harmed—except by my own foolishness. I always felt safe, never afraid. I believed my spirit was with me, guiding and protecting me, and so it was. I also felt safe among the African people, the dark-skinned people. And there was so much to see, discover, and explore—such a rich, authentic life.

Unlike in Europe, nothing was hidden away. Here, life was raw and unfiltered. Death, decay, chaos, stench, noise, and excrement coexisted with laughter, music, dance, playfulness, joy, and an unshakable resilience. People embraced the impermanence of life, knowing we were all just passing through. The powerful Yoruba rhythms pulsed through the streets, driving people to move, create, and fulfill their destinies. Life was intense, vibrant, and pulsating—scorching heat, boundless creativity, deeply rooted spirituality—a dense, overwhelming experience of existence.

It was a stark contrast to Europe's carefully arranged, dollhouse version of life—where everything is neat, predictable, and in its place, and where people live under the illusion of safety and control. And yet, Nigeria had once been a British colony.

Black Lotos

My time in Nigeria left a profound impression on me as if I had returned to an ancient station from my former soul journeys. The deep resonance and understanding I felt were undeniable. After returning to Europe at the end of my third winter in 1990, I decided to establish a legal entity to share the true depth and richness of African cultures—particularly that of the Yoruba—with the public. This decision came from the deepest part of my being, and everything fell into place effortlessly.

I founded a club and named it Black Lotos—"Lotos", symbolizing the sacred flower on which enlightened beings are often depicted in Indian tradition. I attracted Yoruba partners, and together we established a dance theater and music troupe. I organized public festivals, secured funding, and managed all aspects of the project. It was my creation, my passion, my "baby"—and I poured my heart into it completely.

At the time, I was also in a relationship with a Nigerian man, twelve years my junior, whom I had met in Berlin. Naturally, he became part of the project. However, I will leave out the details of this aspect of my personal life for my own reasons.

Our Music Troupe

For nearly ten years, we ran this project. In 1993, I met a Senegalese man who, like us, attended the ISKCON Sunday feast—an event known for its most delicious and heavenly food.

Another Delusion - AMA

Yes, you guessed it right—a love story unfolded between us. For months, we only met at ISKCON, but one day, it became clear that I needed to experience something with him. So, he moved in with me. I knew he had been a heroin addict for ten years but had completed a year-long withdrawal program at a well-known institution and was now clean. He was highly educated, had spent thirteen years as the backbone of the famous Persian Blue Mosque in Hamburg, possessed refined manners, was a poet, and looked stunning. In short, he was my dream man, and I wanted him.

The first four months were unbelievable. He was the most caring and considerate companion I had ever known, and I could hardly believe I was experiencing such love. But then, one day, he began acting strangely. At first, I found his odd behavior amusing and mentioned it to his friend. The friend, however, was immediately alarmed and told me he had relapsed. And he was right.

That's when the hell began. I learned what it was like to live with the demon of heroin in my space. Oh boy, Irena, what next? I moved heaven and earth to help him get clean again, but it was all in vain. After his third relapse, I told him his belongings were in the street where I had placed them and that he should never return. That was it.

From that moment on, I sank into a deep depression, losing all will to live. The light within me went out. I became ill and made no effort to recover—until my Nigerian man came back into my life. At first, he had been furious about my involvement with this man, but he had his own stories—tit for tat. Despite everything, we continued to work together. And now, he came to me, cared for me, stood by my side, and even purchased a piece of land in an incredibly beautiful spot in Nigeria. Slowly, I found my way back. The spirit of our shared project reignited the fire within me.

As for Abdul Aziz, there's something I need to add.

Twenty years later, while living in my father's house in Hamburg and caring for him, my cell phone rang one day. I answered—and instantly recognized the voice. It was my Senegalese delusion of a man. Surprise, surprise! Without hesitation, he asked for my forgiveness in case he had ever done anything to hurt me when we shared our lives together. Hmmm. Forgiven.

Then, he thanked me—for throwing him out of our home. He told me that moment had been the turning point in his life, the moment he truly decided to leave behind the devastation of heroin once and for all. Wow.

But there was more. He revealed that he had lost his sight due to an eye infection, which had led to doctors removing both of his eyeballs. The news left me speechless. Later, I related the entire story to my alcohol-dependent sister, and it shook her to the core.

A few days later, I saw him at Hamburg Airport, where I worked. He was a shadow of the man I once knew—shrunk, uncertain, dependent on someone to guide him. It was a humbling sight. The demon of heroin had once made him believe he was above God.

Blessings on his healing.

A Visit to Ikogosi/BL

Back—or rather forward again—to the project in Nigeria: a journey to Ikogosi. We arrived at the entrance of a vast parking lot for overland taxis and microbuses, alive with bustling activity. Traders moved energetically, carrying their wares—often balanced on their heads or even displayed across their bodies. Mothers breastfed their babies, while children guided blind beggars in their daily "work." Shoes were polished, weary travelers rested their heads on their arms, and vendors offered food, drinks, and everything a traveler might need—or simply desire. Mechanics, with their ingenious improvisation, repaired cars, sometimes using them as makeshift sleeping mats. In short, there was never a dull moment for anyone waiting for their taxi to Akure to fill up and depart—just like us.

As we sat in the relative comfort of our car, traders and beggars took turns approaching us. Old beggars, some blind or crippled, muttered endless prayers in hopes that we would provide for their empty stomachs. Children of all ages sold Coca-Cola, ice water in plastic bags, hard-boiled eggs, biscuits, and bananas. Women offered traditional home-cooked meals from their small roadside stalls, known as bukas. The food was incredibly cheap but rich in flavor—delicious and, of course, fiery hot.

A small man in a gray, woollen suit, adorned with a colorful tie, caught our attention. He was pulling a Christmas turkey behind him on a string. With keen interest, he negotiated the fare with the taxi driver, and then carefully guided his turkey to the front of the car—only for the bird to deliver a well-aimed kick at him. After a brief struggle, the man and the turkey seemed to reach an understanding. The turkey, gasping for air with its beak wide open, shifted nervously from one foot to the other, clearly unsettled. It was obvious—this was its first journey, and it was determined that it would also be its last.

There was so much to take in that I almost felt a tinge of disappointment when I realized we were finally about to leave. Just as I was about to step into the car, I noticed the back tire—smooth as a baby's skin and as flat as an old, worn-out sofa. "Safe journey!" and off we went. Our taxi sputtered, jerked, and stuttered onto the road. The engine, as if shaking off its drowsiness, finally picked up speed and carried us swiftly out of the sprawling metropolis of Lagos onto the highway leading northward.

At last, I could smell my beloved "bush" again—see it, hear it. The land unfolded before me in a vibrant display of colors and shapes. Velvet-green bamboo thickets swayed, towering palm trees cast long, graceful silhouettes, and banana plants unfurled their enormous leaves with urgency. Majestic Iroko trees stood proudly, surrounded by an astonishing variety of other species, all coexisting to create a breathtaking, untamed landscape.

We crossed a river—perhaps four or five times—each crossing different from the last. Sometimes, the water was broad, sluggish, and heavy with silt; other times, it was swift, tumbling over rocks with dexterous agility.

At one point, a colossal rock formation loomed ahead—a primeval giant of ancient granite, shaped and polished over millions of years. It radiated an undeniable power, standing there in silent dignity. I found myself staring, mouth agape, in awe of its sheer presence.

Soon, we arrived in Akure, which seemed to sit upon a plateau. In the early evening haze of the harmattan season, the surrounding mountain range appeared dreamlike—bathed in a misty, golden light.

The streets were filled with people and traffic. Exhausted, we checked into our hotel, refreshed ourselves, and collapsed onto our beds. Unfortunately, our room was directly adjacent to the bar, where blaring music and television persisted throughout the night, only to start again at dawn, precisely at 5:30 a.m.

The next morning, around 11 a.m., we resumed our journey. The sun, already high in the sky, burned down relentlessly. Our taxi—chartered for the trip—was packed to the brim with supplies we had acquired in Akure: mattresses, water containers, shovels, hoes for the construction site, and more. We barely had enough room to squeeze in.

As we left the town, the road became a slalom course, weaving around countless potholes. Again and again, we found ourselves facing oncoming traffic head-on, dodging past by mere millimeters. The further we traveled, the steeper the terrain became. Before long, the landscape unfolded into rolling hills—lush, vibrant, and full of life.

Then, at last, we saw a sign announcing our destination: Ikogosi. The road twisted and turned, climbing uphill before dipping down again. With each valley we crossed, my anticipation grew. My neck stretched longer and longer as I strained for the first glimpse of the town.

Finally, after cresting one last hill, we saw it—first, a scattering of houses, then a wide valley unfurling before us, cradling its hidden jewel: Ikogosi. Would this be my future home? At that moment, I had no idea that it held a population of 20,000. To me, it seemed like nothing more than a small, tranquil village.

As we entered, we passed the taxi stand—but curiously, there were no taxis in sight. The king's palace stood ahead, but it was surprisingly modest, a humble structure in contrast to the towering church behind it, which was a hundred times its size.

At the next corner, we passed the home of the old hunter who had sold us the land. He was rumored to be a ruthless man. The road curved slightly and then sloped gently downward. Women and children approached, balancing heavy buckets and basins of water on their heads with effortless grace.

As we stopped and stepped out, we were instantly surrounded by children. They came running from the quarters where we would be staying, eager to help carry in our belongings.

Our room was square, with a window that framed our hill. It was mostly empty except for a few wooden ledges along the walls. We swept the floor, laid our mattresses directly on the bare cement, attempted to arrange our belongings, and made ourselves at home.

The men were busy, so I set off on an inquisitive first exploration. The view from the terrace of our home was enchanting in the truest sense of the word. The silence was intoxicating—broken only by the chirping of countless crickets and the varied songs of birds, as if they, in their diversity, were attempting to enforce the hush. Rows of beautiful hills lined up beside one another, drawing my gaze toward the valley below, where dense bushes grew along the roadside.

Swiftly, I discovered the source of all this thick, lush greenery: a lively, clear rivulet carrying cool water through the land, sustaining all forms of life. By the water's edge, I found a gathering of women and children—washing clothes, fetching water, and bathing right there. They eyed me with astonishment; some greeted me in English, and they were visibly surprised when I responded in Yoruba. (This was my seventh trip to Nigeria, and I had already spent more than two years living in various parts of the country.) Word spread quickly throughout the village: Oyinbo (redface) speaks Yoruba!

Continuing my walk, I reached the blue gate of Ikogosi Warm Springs. In front of it, the rivulet ran beneath the street and veered off to the left. I stepped past the gate into government-designated territory, marked by a fence running parallel to the road.

I drank in the multitude of sensations—the deep green of the landscape, the cheerful murmur of the flowing water beside me, the chorus of crickets, and the many birds calling, some in lively chatter, others as if whispering cryptic messages in rhythmic tones. The oppressiveness of the city fell away from me, and I knew I was home. The heat enveloped me like a protective shield, and I had already "landed" there, embracing Ikogosi completely, with all its consequences.

The next day, we set out to visit the former sacred shrine of the goddess, the giver of the hot and cold springs. The shrine was nestled in a cool hollow of the valley, surrounded by towering ancient trees, their crowns forming a natural canopy. In this secluded grove, the hot and cold springs merged. A series of steps led up to the source itself, about 20 meters high. The steps had been cemented—perhaps for protection—and some unsightly concrete pipes extended down into the valley.

The goddess of the springs, after enduring repeated exploitation of her gift of salt by the local inhabitants, had withdrawn. The festival once held in her honor—when she provided protection in times of war and healing in times of peace—had long ceased and is expected to be observed only in secret. Stealthily, those who still felt connected to her, come to pay homage, for Christianity has entered Ikogosi, with various sects preaching progress along European lines. Who would dare to publicly honor the old goddess now?

On my way back to the entrance gate, I passed a swimming pool filled with water from the hot spring, offering a truly unique bathing experience. It was a proper pool, lined with tiles, measuring about 120–150 cm deep and 5 by 10 meters in size. Around it, tables and chairs were arranged for visitors. After my first swim, I felt completely at home—both within myself and in this place. During our three-month stay, I spent most of my time in that hot pool, almost melting away. Well—there was much to melt away in my field.

There is also a small zoo in the area—once beautifully designed but now completely neglected. Only a rusty old sign remains, a fading reminder that lions, crocodiles, turtles, water birds, and monkeys once lived here. Now, the bush has reclaimed the territory, and no one cares for this forgotten place. Two abandoned crocodiles have been left to vegetate alone for years, unfed. Is this a challenge for us?

I sat on the veranda of our small, humble dwelling. The house owner was cutting the tall grass with his massive bush knife. His son arrived with a small dish of kerosene, and, piece by piece, the vast land in front of the house was set ablaze. The flames roared with impressive might, crackling loudly as they consumed the dried-out bush—a raw display of nature's power. Within minutes, only thin columns of smoke drifted with the wind over the scorched, barren earth. The snakes had vanished. The land lay charred. A small tree drooped, its roasted leaves hanging in sadness. A lone cricket fled from the dead grass, rubbing its legs in loud protest.

Once every hour, a car rushed past while pedestrians came and went in large groups, balancing heavy loads on their heads.

The peace and stillness deepened as SunRa climbed higher in the sky. The midday heat spread an oppressive weight, slowing all movement to a crawl. Too sluggish to write, I retreated to my room and collapsed onto the bed.

That was in 1996. I had seen the project site, and yes, we had begun building our village. It was nestled in gently mountainous terrain, surrounded by lush vegetation, moderate temperatures, and stifling humidity. I spent weeks soaking in the hot pool, letting the rushing water and the mysterious calls of hidden birds soothe my soul. Above me, monkeys played the fool in the trees.

We spent three months monitoring the construction. But our relationship had lost its depth—we quarreled often, and somehow, the spark was gone. Eventually, it was time to return to Berlin before the house was completed. The money had run out, and the structure was left without a roof.

The villagers—a dubious lot, except for the traditional king with whom we shared many sweet social moments—had their own plans. After the rainy season, the building was completely destroyed. Rain? Or something else?

On the journey back, I had a clear realization: this would be my last visit to Nigeria and the Yoruba people, with whom I had once shared a deep, ancient connection.

The First Building I Design and It's Built without Cement

And This Is How It Ends – We Decide To Leave This Alien Village

See-saw, see-saw—that's how life goes. One moment, it's full of promise; the next, everything is gone… over and over again. I am tired.

Some More Pictures of Our Creative Festival Contributions:

A Play about Slavery

We Are Having Lots of Fun

Here We Are Sharing Dinner with Our Wonderful Sudanese Friends, Who Have Joined Us in Some of Our Performances

I must highlight one aspect of life in Berlin that I deeply enjoyed—the House of World Cultures in the heart of Tiergarten. It gifted me countless hours of admiring inspiring cultural expressions from all corners of the world, spanning every genre: performances, theatre, music, art exhibitions, events, and the World Disco. Its architecture is striking, resembling a massive oyster. Inside, a spacious open area unfolds beneath its undulating roof—simply beautiful.

It became almost my second home. I spent so much time there, relishing walks through the surrounding forest and eagerly approaching this remarkable structure, always in suspense about what it would unveil next for Berlin's public. For many years, it was world-class—undeniably the best. The experience was unforgettable and profoundly inspiring. Africa, India, China—oh yes, the Chinese opera—absolutely wonderful! Live music to dance to, an endless variety of soul-nurturing and sense-awakening performances. Thank you to all the incredible creative muses!

Regarding our Black Lotus project, public funds were channeled into Berlin, but our relationship soured over time. Eventually, I decided to bring the project to a close and reclaim my own personal path and interests. It took me five years to let go of my obsession with establishing something in Nigeria—especially with a man who, as it turned out, had a secret life besides using me for his own selfish interests. I hold no resentment toward him, for I played along, failing to acknowledge my own blind spots in our relationship.

Finally, in 2001, with much pain in my heart, I put an end to this disastrous chapter. But as one door closed, the future opened up for me once again.

Now, I had to design a completely new life, as the old one lay in ruins before me. It was time to turn my back on Africa, leave it to its own fate, and focus on myself. Yet, another deep black hole loomed ahead. Who? What? Where? This was the moment I had finally freed myself from the burdens I had carried for so long.

And this is my legacy to my beloved:

Africa, Old Africa

Remind us who we really are!
We have been misled, unplugged,
Yes, humankind has all been mugged
Of its true grandeur at large
Since false gods have taken charge.
They feed on weakness and our fears,
Find joy in murder and human tears.
Let us put a stop to this,
In that we learn to realize
Just who, by nature, we really are.
Power over, power under—few are up, most suffer yonder,
Gave their charge to those who lead, feeding them in all their greed.
Humans, take your power back!
Know thyselves, leave those quacks!
Dive down into your inner Selves,
Pay no heed to what society tells.
Seek thy own knowing and thy truth;
There you'll find eternal youth.
Seek peace and love and harmony;
Cease to fall for that game of split-party.
An eye for an eye, a tooth for a tooth?
It's a man for a girl now, elders for youth!
That old game of separation is over;
There is a much better one to discover.
Do thy task now, and do it well;

Evolve yourself out of the false god's spell.
Old paradigm breaking off—new game's name is light and love!

Africa, old mother of ours,
Teach us again our inherited powers!
Build this planet back to its splendor;
Teach your children to surrender
To the needs we feel at this time:
The vibrations of love and compassion,
Of truth and creation, of wisdom and light.

IsIs, March 1997

For the time being, I turn my back on you and your powerful people who have it in them to adjust their society without my help! Your gift to me during my time in the bush of Iragbiji has remained the most naturally blissful of my experiences, and I am filled with gratitude for this priceless gift. Thank you, Mama Africa!

Turning to Me Again - Berlin

With the onset of menopause in 2000, that peculiar practice of "rabbit sex" came to an end for me as well. What remained was a deep-seated addiction to people, a longing to belong somewhere, and a need for acknowledgment.

In an unconscious attempt to fill the void within me after leaving Africa, I sought out communities where I could live and immerse myself in various spiritual groups. However, each resonated only for a while before I moved on. Here's a chronological journey of my experiences:

- In 1999, I found myself outside Berlin near a community called the Centre for Experimental Creation of Society, hoping to explore a new way of life. However, I was immediately put off when men seemed to expect a "bed tax" from potential partners. Despite this, I stayed for a while because I lived in the forest, reconnecting with my beloved nature. I participated in a free school project but soon realized that this was not my path—too much headache! So, I returned to Berlin.
- Damanhur, a spiritual community in the Italian Alps with its stunning temple carved into the rock, was inspired by ancient Pharaonic Egypt. While visiting the place around 2000, I sensed strange, energetic undercurrents that made me uneasy. Ultimately, I decided it was not for me.
- During my time at Brahma Kumaris World Spiritual University (BKWSU) (1999 – 2002), I experienced healing and learned many valuable teachings. However, I eventually left due to their unscientific belief in a 5,000-year cycle of repetition. A senior member once told me I should dedicate my life to enlightenment because I was ready for it. I jokingly responded that I would attain liberation when my hair turned completely silver—which, as of now, is about the time!
- I studied sacred geometry, numerology, alchemy, homeopathy, astrology, and reincarnation through regression

methods. I explored the science of magic, the Kabbalah, and a bit of Tantra. I became a member of the German Society of Spiritual Healers, offering distant healing by prayer—free of charge—and with successful outcomes. I also taught myself Jin Shin Jyutsu, a Japanese healing art, and practised it extensively. My former lifestyle of sex, drugs, and rock 'n' roll effortlessly faded away when I turned to meditation and spiritual disciplines in 1983.

- I followed the teachings of Babaji of Herakhan, embracing the principles of "Truth, Simplicity, and Love" (1984).
- I did a Shamanic Training with the Dear Tribe Métis Medicine Society Native American Nation's guidance from 1997 to 1999.

I first encountered ISKCON (Hare Krishna) devotees at Lagos Airport in 1988, to my great surprise. We had a long and fascinating conversation. Since 1992, I have attended their Sunday public feasts almost every week for years, savoring their exquisite, Krishna-blessed Ayurvedic cuisine. During this time, I nearly delved into reading the Mahabharata and found immense joy not just in the divine food but also in the Vedic teachings, cultural performances, public celebrations, and more.

At some point, I decided to confront my claustrophobic fear of sweat lodges. I had heard that once inside, participants were not allowed to leave during the ceremony. Determined, I found a woman who conducted sweat lodge ceremonies in nature by one of the many lakes around Berlin. She assured me that it was possible to exit during one of the four pauses when fresh water was brought in, and more heated rocks were added. Encouraged by this, I took the plunge, embracing what would become the first of many such experiences—hundreds, in fact! It turned out to be a profound treat for the body, soul, and spirit.

The ceremony itself is an immersive experience. It begins early in the afternoon with a gathering to dig the fire pit, set up the lodge around it, and cover it with blankets. We then sit on the earth and participate in a "talking stick" circle, where each person introduces themselves and shares their intentions for the ceremony. As the talking stick is passed around, the rule is simple: only the person holding it can speak while everyone else listens attentively—no interruptions, no discussions. Then, Uta explains the process and answers any questions. Every action is imbued with prayer and preceded by invocations to the powers of Nature and the Spirit world, creating a deeply spiritual and transformative experience.

Then—finally—the time arrived for the actual ceremony, ideally at dusk. The fire had been lit, heating the rocks until they glowed. People gathered, undressing completely before lining up in front of the lodge. One by one, Uta smudged each of us with sacred smoke, and in silence, we crawled on all fours into the lodge. As we crossed the threshold, we whispered a prayer: "For all my ancestors." I turned left, following the circular path to my place, until everyone, including Uta and a bucket of water, was inside. The doormat was lowered, and pitch-black darkness enveloped us.

Uta began calling in the powers—one by one—a long succession of invocations to the elements, the stars, the moon, the beings of the upper and lower worlds, the unborn, the deceased, the ancestors, the ascended masters, and finally, WakanTanka, the Great Spirit. These invocations infuse the space with their presence, both around and within us. Uta's voice carried them with gentleness and reverence, and I loved the way they flowed effortlessly from her tongue.

Now, water was poured onto the hot rocks in the central pit, and steam rose, condensing on our skin, taking our breath away for a moment before we surrendered to the experience. Each of the four rounds carried a different theme. After each round, the doormat was lifted, a fresh bucket of water was brought in, sometimes more hot rocks, and then the darkness of the mother's womb swallowed us once again. This was a time of intense prayer, meditation, speaking to WakanTanka, and listening to That Grand Black Unknown. Deep purification took place, and at the end of the ceremony, the powers were released one by one with gratitude.

Finally, the doormat was lifted, and in reverse order, we crawled out of the lodge. In winter, we rolled naked in the snow; in summer, we dipped into the cold lake just a few meters away. Our steaming bodies felt transformed, vibrating with a profound stillness. Slowly, we dressed and silently shared the food and drink we had brought. Then, we went straight home—no socializing that night—just resting in that energy and drifting into a blissful sleep.

The next morning, we met again—late. It was time to take down the lodge, dry the blankets in the sun, clean the fire pit, stack the rocks, and clear the space. Then came the most important part: the "talking stick" sharing round. Each of us shared our experiences—an absolute feast of stories, revealing how Spirit had moved through us all. I cherished these rounds—times of raw truth beyond value. In those moments, everyone felt like a part of me.

I was so drawn to these ceremonies that I enroled in a two-year training course with Uta. We met weekly in a group to learn and practice an array of powerful rituals, including more and more sweat lodges. All of this wisdom comes from the Dear Tribe Métis Medicine Society (DTMMS), based in Flagstaff, Arizona. Also known as the Twisted Hairs, this lineage weaves together the ancient knowledge of various Native American tribal nations into a single teaching—a treasury of practical wisdom.

One year, I participated in the renowned SunDance ceremony. This took us to Southern France for a week, and the ritual began immediately, lasting the entire time. First, we set up the round space for the dance, deep in nature. This sacred space is called the Arbor, and at its center stands the tree towards which the dancers move before returning to their respective resting places—where they remain for three full days and nights, like the rays of SunRa.

The music and drums are then prepared, including a massive drum large enough for eight people to sit around it. I volunteered as one of the drummers. During the core of the ceremony—the actual SunDance—that drum is beaten continuously, 24/7, for the full three days and nights.

We set up our individual tents and stowed away our belongings. A large kitchen tent was erected, and the dining tent was set up right beside it. Some folks were setting up small stalls to sell their handcrafted jewelry, dreamcatchers, clothing, sage, pāua shells, feathers, and more.

During the ceremony, relentless rain poured down for days as if trying to wash us away—turning the entire place into a chaotic mudslide. But then, SunRa had mercy on us, drying up the muck, and we were finally able to enjoy the beautiful experience. Radiantly happy faces filled our hearts as we parted ways and traveled back home. Thank you, WakanTanka!

During a weekend training on Medicine Wheels for women, during the final sweat lodge, I asked for and received my Native American medicine name: Eagle Who Flies in the Dawn. I believe it truly marked the beginning of a new phase in my life. (2018)

Looking back at 2002—oh God! In my 25 years of living in Berlin, I moved house 24 times! Unbelievable how mobile I was—or was it restlessness? More likely! And I still am (2021).

It was a deeply confusing time for me. I was searching, though I was not sure for what. I found things, discarded them, and kept searching. I had long since thrown out my TV, replacing it with books in a desperate attempt to find clarity—only to end up feeling even more lost. I tried to start a business but never succeeded, lacking a true inner passion for anything.

During a period of unemployment, I poured my energy into creating hundreds of mandalas from plaster of paris. Day after day, I sat at home, my mind consumed by frustration and inner turmoil, hoping that the creative process would heal me and lead me to inner peace.

But I had no luck selling them—only the children loved them, captivated by their bright colors.

I often felt as if I were teetering on the edge of madness in this utterly rootless existence. The foreign culture around me, the disconnect from nature, from my true self, from spirit, from the world itself—I felt like a lost child, desperately scrambling for security, orientation, and my place in this world. And my purpose in it.

For the first time, I became fully aware of my fragmented inner state, a wound I had carried since childhood. It terrified me—I was not ready to face it. I only felt disconnected and drowning in despair. It seemed as though love had no place in this world.

All the meditation and spiritual reading did not seem to help at the time. So, I returned to my first profession as a kindergarten teacher and trained in Montessori pedagogy—a method I thoroughly enjoyed. How I wished I had been fortunate enough to learn about life this way when I was a child!

I found work at an international Montessori kindergarten for diplomats, where English was the primary language. It was a rewarding opportunity to serve, grow, and improve myself for the sake of those beautiful little souls from all over the world. With only 24 children in the group, we could truly attend to each child's individual needs, creating a peaceful, enriching learning environment.

Working with children was a healing and grounding experience—one that brought me back to a sense of purpose.

Montessori PreSchool in Dahlem, Berlin, 2003-2005

I practically have no "private life" beyond continuing my studies and gradually letting go of my African past, along with everything I had accumulated—mostly musical instruments. I had studied books to reconnect with what had long been buried deep within my soul—clothes and various artifacts. I consciously separate myself from my African past to be fully free for whatever comes next—whether it be experience, research, or exploration.

Grunewald Fun (left), Playing the Devil in Hell for a Kid's Project (right)

EGYPT – Africa, Here I Come Again!

I was inspired by an African-American friend who was studying Egyptology. I often visited him at the Egyptology Institute of FU Berlin, which was conveniently close to both my home and workplace. Over several months, I spent many days there—scouring the library, engaging in discussions, debating various topics, and listening to his insights. I was captivated. Something within me was powerfully awakened. A fire was reignited!

EGYPT. EGYPT. EGYPT – It felt like a natural next step—another ancient part of Africa with its rich spiritual traditions calling to me.

I soon immersed myself in the works of Christian Jacq, an Egyptologist dismissed by his mainstream colleagues. Instead of pursuing strict academic writing, he transformed his deep admiration and extensive knowledge of ancient Egypt into popular novels. I devoured them, lost myself in their pages, and forgot the world around me. Something deep inside stirred that fire once more. I enjoyed my job to some extent, but I knew it was not my final destination. I felt restless, stuck, and ready for a change.

By May 2005, Berlin was still covered in snow, and the weather was cold and wet. Summer seemed distant, and I had grown tired of this perpetual state of waiting—for warmth, for sunlight, for something more. I had enough. It was time. I made my decision: I was leaving these latitudes for good. I booked a flight to Cape Town, South Africa, returning to the land I had left 30 years earlier—now free from Apartheid. At the same time, I planned a three-week trip to Luxor, Upper Egypt—the ancient capital of Upper and Lower Egypt for over a thousand years, once known as Thebes, "The City of Palaces." I needed to see and feel the places that had so deeply resonated with me through Christian Jacq's novels.

In July 2005, I boarded a massive jumbo jet for the 12-hour journey to South Africa. It was winter there. As I waited to board, I marveled at the sight of the plane being loaded—tons of luggage, food, fuel, and passengers. How, I wondered, did this heavy bird manage to take off and stay in the air with all that weight?

Settling into my seat, I hoped the one next to me would remain empty. But no—someone had their eye on it. I glanced at him and thought, Hmm, better keep your distance, buddy. I tried to give off unwelcoming vibes, but he did not care. He sat down. Scruffy, lean, and slightly gaunt, he wore dark, casual clothes that hung loosely on his frame.

Resigning myself to the fact that I'd have to tolerate his presence for the next 12 hours, I braced for the long flight. But as the journey progressed, we began talking—first casually, then more openly, sharing pieces of our lives. Before long, we realized we had a common interest. He was planning a project on his farm near Cape Town, and it seemed there might be a way for me to contribute. By the time we approached landing, we had agreed to meet so he could show me his farm.

I had a wonderful time in Cape Town, staying with a Facebook friend who shared my interest in spirituality. The house was lovely, with a garden and a pool, providing me with both safety and happiness. I ventured out to explore the city. Since I was staying in a small town outside of Cape Town, I took the train into the city. Unaware of the class divisions in the train system, I boarded a third-class carriage, which was packed with so-called "colored" and Black South Africans.

As I looked around, I studied the faces and smiles of the people that invited connection. My presence stood out, and people approached me, curious about where I was from because it was clear that I was not a white South African who would not dare take the train, much less ride in a third-class carriage or, heaven forbid, smile at fellow passengers. We exchanged stories, and I made friends easily—surrounded by open-hearted, welcoming faces. There was no hostility, no tension, just a sense of human connection. It was wonderful.

Another time, I traveled into town by car, passing by a so-called "township" of Cape Colored people. What I saw left me horrified. The sheer poverty and misery were beyond words. Even now, I struggle to describe the scene. It tore at my heart. And yet, right next to this suffering stood massive villas—luxurious estates overflowing with excess. The stark contrast was staggering, leaving me speechless.

I knew the history. I had seen how these people had been enslaved, exploited, and brainwashed into believing they were inferior and undeserving of anything better. Rage welled up inside me. How could such injustice exist? How could people be so heartless?

Yet, from a higher perspective, I wondered—could this suffering be part of a greater cosmic compassion? A call for these downtrodden souls to remember their innate divinity and rise beyond their oppression? They say a hungry man is an angry man, yet these people seemed to have given up. Many had sunk into despair, feeling like outcasts, belonging nowhere. The Cape Coloured community, in particular, had been stripped of their cultural heritage—rejected by both their black and white ancestors. Their fate was truly heart-wrenching. Life is a mystery.

And yes, I felt compelled to act, to do something meaningful to uplift people. I thought about the farm owned by my fellow passenger from the plane. There was not much to see—a few buildings and vast land stretching toward the sea, with gentle hills rolling beyond. But there was potential. We agreed to meet there again in January 2006, after my journey to Egypt.

South Africa—here I come.

Back in Germany, I wrapped up my life once again. I sold and gave away my belongings, resigned from my beloved job, and gave up my apartment. On December 1st, I boarded a plane bound for LUXOR, EGYPT.

As I left the airport, I was enchanted by the sights and sensations around me.

Said was waiting for me. After we boarded the family car, he drove me to a small hotel run by his brother. His name, Said, means "happy," and true to its meaning, we laughed, joked, and enjoyed the ride. I already felt at home.

We traveled along a canal for quite some distance, with palm trees waving their arms at me and donkeys trotting along, resigned to their head-hanging fate. The men wore long, elegant gowns called galabiyas, while the few women in sight were draped in pitch-black robes, covering them from head to toe—a reflection of the farmers' way of life.

At last, I was embraced by the abundant sunlight and comforting warmth. The deep blue sky stretched endlessly above, while a friendly and welcoming atmosphere surrounded me. I loved it!

We crossed the Nile via the only bridge in southern Luxor. The river was broad, and the bridge was long. To the south, flat, low-lying fruit fields extended to the desert's edge. On the West Bank, we rode north along another canal, where vibrant acacia flamboyant trees, adorned with fiery red blossoms, lined the road. Endless bushes of Bougainvillea flourished in a dazzling variety of colors, blessed by the light of Sun Ra. I was captivated!

Vast sugarcane fields alternated with maize crops and lush greenery, providing food for the donkeys. Along the opposite side of the canal stood small, humble mud houses—the homes of the fellahin, the local farmers. Gradually, more signs of human settlement appeared, signaling our arrival at Luxor West Bank.

We soon passed the Murur, a police checkpoint at the bridge, and entered Gezira—the part of Luxor that sits on the shores of the Nile, that grand life-giver upon which all existence depends in this arid, barren land. Just before we reached the river, near the ferry anchorage and the parking lot teeming with motorboats, we veered right onto a dirt road leading southward along the riverbank. A final turn and two houses down the road, we arrived at my destination: Senmut Hotel, where I had booked myself for my Luxorian re-membrance adventure.

I was taken up to the rooftop, where I was greeted with a breath-taking view of Luxor East Bank—the city proper—with the magnificent Luxor Temple standing proudly across the river. Wow.

Then, I turned around—and oh, shock! A sudden, dramatic, heart-opening experience struck me like a thunderbolt—BOOM!

I heard myself exclaim aloud, "This is the place where I will live and die!"

Oh my God! My entire being was on fire! I felt blessed, overwhelmed with bliss. I had come home. Thebes—oh, Thebes! The ancient dwelling of my soul from three and a half thousand years ago and countless times before. No words could capture what I felt.

It was clear—I had to abandon my plans to move to Cape Town. I made the call, and the man on the other end was very understanding. He simply said, "You must follow your heart. Good luck, and fare well!"

It felt right. There was nothing left to do but act on it!

During these first three weeks, I delved into my ancient past and explored the temples, beginning with the workers' village of Deir El Medina and the small Eirene Temple behind it. I had a profound experience there—when I stepped onto the granite slab beneath the temple's entrance, I was hit with an overwhelming verbal download, a rush of information too fast to grasp. Startled, I quickly jumped off. Uff!

Deir El Medina

At that time, my mind was still caught up in its constant chatter, so I was not particularly sensitive to vibrations or energies. However, I did notice that wherever I went, men were paying me a bit too much attention for my liking. To be honest, a part of me enjoyed being seen as a woman again—something that had long faded in Europe, where men only seemed to notice young, skinny girls, Barbie-like figures in high heels, an image I never identified with. So, while I basked in the attention, I kept my distance, staying vigilant. It was all too clear what "marriage" meant to them—no, thank you. I had no interest in becoming a bed-bound donkey. I happily slept alone. Still, I enjoyed the playful game; it added a bit of excitement to life. After all, I am a Leo girl!

Time and time again, I found myself in awe of the temples—the immaculate precision, the perfect beauty and harmony of the inscriptions, the hieroglyphs, the colossal granite sculptures, and the intricate designs of both temples and tombs. And the sheer scale of it all—wow! What incredible spirits had built this? And what even greater spirits had planned it?

Ramses II, the last great Pharaoh, is completely misinterpreted by mainstream Egyptology!

Abydos Temple of Seti I, the Most Beautiful and Fine Temple Work (left); Ramses II in Luxor Temple, the Last Great Pharao (right)

I can only encourage readers to visit these ancient sites—monumental testaments to our true innate human potential and a source of inspiration to revive it once more. Egypt stands as the world's foremost cultural heritage treasure and one of the most visited destinations globally. Is it true? I wonder. But it certainly ranks among the top.

Back to My Reality

I returned to Berlin in December 2005, only to board another plane bound for Windhoek, South West Africa. On that freezing, snowy night, the plane had to be defrosted before taking off for Namibia, where I had committed to babysitting for 12 days. My destination was a luxury farm owned by wealthy people, surrounded by electric fences—protection from the "wildlife" outside. There, I was to care for a lost and lonely, spoiled little girl.

Her father spent his days hunting that very "wildlife," returning with his trophies, beaming with pride. Many a powerful and beautiful kudu lost its life. Her mother was a restless, talkative, and controlling woman who had long since abandoned herself. I found myself counting the days, then the hours, but instead of passing quickly, they seemed to stretch endlessly. Oh my. "Patience is the mother of joy," they say, but what a challenge it is to be around people so detached from reality—trapped in their own little fantasy world, possessing everything money can buy yet lacking even a simple smile in the morning. Lord, have mercy on me! A replay of my own family scenario.

South West Africa was once a German colony, and even today, some forgotten German folk still celebrate Hitler's birthday every year—a sour, lingering atmosphere, palpable even now.

Namibia is a vast, empty land where dry savanna and desert alternate endlessly. We traveled across it on our way to Swakopmund to spend a few days at the coast—an experience that failed to excite me. And, to my disappointment, no photo safari in the famous Etosha Pan was planned. I know this sounds ungrateful, but it was how I felt. Finally, the long-awaited day arrived: time to board my flight back to Berlin. Goodbye at last! Relief washed over me.

Then, on January 19, 2006, I was off to Luxor—to stay! Huurraayyy!

Nile & Fruitland Egypt

Dream of Living on the Banks of the Nile

I leaped without a safety net, relying only on the grace of my ORI. Leaving behind the predictable, cozy, yet dull and empty life in Berlin was all that mattered. With little money in my purse or bank account, I landed in the home of a Belgian woman of my age. She had married a young, tall, and handsome Egyptian man who was helping her build a stunning villa in the fields of Thebes West Bank, near the grand temple of Medinet Habu and the Qurn—the pyramid-shaped mountain peak that hides the Valley of the Kings.

It was the tourist attraction of Luxor, and back then, tourism was still thriving!

In those days, the entire mountain range, stretching from Qurn to the northern entrance of the same Kings Valley, was inhabited by local people who had lived there for centuries without electricity or running water. Water had to be carried up in tanks by donkeys.

People lived in simple, unadorned mud houses with high ceilings designed for better air circulation, eliminating the need for air conditioning or other modern conveniences. Life was centered around communal and family circles, deeply rooted in ancient customs and traditions. They lived simple yet fulfilling lives, tending to their fields below the mountain and caring for their animals—donkeys, cows, and buffaloes.

But let me return to my story. I was happy to live in such a beautiful and auspicious place near the mountain, trusting that everything else would fall into place in due time.

During the early days of my stay among the fellahin on the West Bank, I spent most of my time with Ahmed, one of the brothers of Said, who had warmly welcomed me at the airport. Ahmed owned a small white car and would take me to various villages to meet people in need of healing. I would lay my hands—blessed with a powerful healing gift—upon them, connect with the Divine within, and pray for their ailments to be cured. The joy and satisfaction I felt upon seeing them relax and smile after my work was immeasurable. I never charged for my healing services, yet they were often met with great success. Occasionally, I received farm produce as a token of gratitude, which I gladly accepted and shared with Ahmed's family.

I spent much of my time in their large family home, where the father, mother, and four of their sons lived with their wives and children under one roof. The parents resided in the basement, while each son occupied a flat above with his family. Three sisters lived with their husbands in surrounding villages, one son had been lost to Austria, and one sister, who worked as a lawyer, lived with the parents downstairs. Altogether, Allah had blessed this local Khadi and his wife with ten children.

As a local Khadi, the father was responsible for officiating marriages. Those seeking to wed came to him to have their contracts signed and complete the formal administrative process. Often, the family also provided, furnished, and hosted the wedding ceremonies and celebrations in their spacious garden. Highly respected throughout Luxor, the father worked diligently to uphold the family's reputation. He was a strict and rigid man, burdened by suppressed emotions, which had left the left side of his body nearly paralyzed. I treated him several times, but he remained unwavering in his ways. He upheld traditions without question—custom was custom.

Rarely did he leave the house for work. Instead, from dawn to dusk, he kept a watchful eye on all the movements within the household, closely monitoring the comings and goings of his children and grandchildren.

Ahmed was a kind but utterly confused man, living under the dictum of his father while still playing that game—the one the Saidis play—enticing older women like me into giving them "good" sex in exchange for generous payment. He was creative, but what could he do with his creativity? There was no guidance, no direction. So, he found his own way to express his frustration.

At the family home, everyone would gather in the large basement hall for meals—wives, children, grandparents, and, eventually, me as well. I was soon to be a wife, though a very different one. He would place himself strategically near the door, where everyone had to pass, armed with a long cane. Each time one of the other wives walked by, he would bring the stick down on her backside—smack!—making them jump and squeal. I watched this for some time. Then, one day, I stood up, wrestled the stick from his hands, and turned the game around. This time, the cane danced on his backside—smack, smack, smack! Oh, how he ran! And oh, how the women, including Grandma, applauded! That was the end of that game.

Egyptian Cooking Is Natural, Healthy and Delicious – and Smells for Miles of Tons of Garlic!

I often observed how sisters were smacked in the face whenever they spoke uncomfortable truths. Once, I saw a grown man bend down to the level of a little girl, seize her face, and force a long, deep kiss onto her poor, helpless mouth. I did not know who he was—father, brother, uncle, or neighbor—but I knew what I had witnessed: the early indoctrination of male sexual domination and abuse.

When I speak of the Egyptians, I specifically refer to the Upper Egyptian Fellahin—the farmers. My understanding comes from first-hand experience, having lived among them for over five years, closely observing their distinct way of life.

Saidis Are Great Brothers to Each Other! They Never Grow up!

Jokes about them made the rounds, as is the case in all nations. I will call them Saidis, as that is how they referred to themselves—always with a broad, unmistakable Saidi grin, radiating their simple yet profound sense of humor. "Saidi" means "merry" or "happy," and their humor was indeed their most striking characteristic—at least to someone coming from Germany. They had a playful way of connecting, purely for the joy of sharing a smile, a joke, laughter, or even just a few kind or silly words—the subtle fabric that weaves human culture. Among themselves, they exchanged elaborate greeting rituals that ebbed and flowed like ocean waves, crashing onto the shore only to be drawn back and return again.

Ali, the Waterman, Look at His Naughty Expression!

One day, I finally decided to climb the Qurn. I dragged Ahmed out of bed earlier than usual (for him), and we hopped into a local taxi that took us to the ticket office. From there, we hiked up the mountain to the intermediate platform, where the police were stationed—a place that reeked like a public toilet because, in fact, it was one. Püh! We hurried past, eager to reach the next level, attempting to climb the great rocky nose at the top. We did not make it. But the breath-taking view that unfolded before us was well worth the effort! I wanted to stay there forever, embraced by the stillness. I felt connected to the "Goddess Who Loves the Stillness," the mighty cobra who once resided there, bestowing wisdom upon those initiated ages ago.

Eventually, we descended back into the village, where we stopped at a humble foul joint run by an old man. We enjoyed a hearty breakfast of foul (beans) with hot butter—hmmm, delicious!

The View from the Top of the Pyramid "Qurn", See the Knee?

The Saidis lived according to deeply ingrained traditions rooted in an ancient past, blended with the nomadic spirit of desert wanderers and the rugged yet devout ways of Islam, which seemed tailor-made for their kind of people. Observing and taking part in their daily lives was an enriching experience. They had preserved simple yet harmonious ways of cooperating within their community. Their hospitality was remarkable—warm, unpretentious, and deeply human. However, one had to remain alert when dealing with them, for selflessness was not a defining trait among them. But then again, where is it these days?

Children were not raised under strict discipline but instead grew naturally into the life they found around them, shaped by the extended family and community-oriented lifestyle. Peer groups were formed organically, and if anything, it was the children who taught each other how to navigate the world—somewhat reminiscent of Black African communities, yet distinctly different. It is still common for three or four generations to live under the same roof. Children are regarded as gifts from God, and a man's ability to father many is a source of patriarchal pride. Having a dozen children with one wife was once the norm, though among the younger generation, economic realities have shifted this trend to just two. And since Muslim men can marry up to four wives, the number of children in a single family can still be astonishingly high. Life, for them, revolves around the extended family—a vast and intricate network of kinship and tradition.

Money has become an ever-elusive prize, pursued by all means—ethical or not—to satisfy the countless desires fueled by television and the internet, now omnipresent in nearly every household. People abandon their once simple and content lives to chase after more—more wealth, more status, more possessions.

The older generation is fading fast, having spent their strength and years shouldering the weight of responsibility for their countless offspring. Their lives were defined by grueling labor in the fields and an unyielding adherence to ancient, restrictive traditions.

They practice a kind of vendetta—if one family member is killed, revenge demands the death of someone from the opposing family. And so the cycle of bloodshed continues endlessly.

Their world has been forcibly thrust into the 21st century, shaken by the devastating impact of the High Dam on agriculture, rigid religious-political doctrines, the fluctuations of the global economy, and the steady erosion of their long-held ways.

True education—the kind that shapes individuals into well-rounded human beings—is virtually non-existent. Yet, it is desperately needed to replace the deeply ingrained, out-dated values of the old patriarchal society.

As farmers, their concerns revolve around food, trade, family, shelter, and social standing within their community. The values that once held their society together now seem obsolete. If culture exists at all, it is steadily crumbling into nothingness. As individuals, people are lost, struggling through the darkest nights of their souls. The painful process of individuation is taking hold, manifesting in an imbalanced and chaotic transformation across all aspects of life.

Disconnected from themselves, they drift like leaves in the wind, living aimless lives dictated by materialistic desires, primal instincts, and narrow perspectives. Trapped between the old and the new, they face overwhelming challenges, as is the case in many parts of the world.

Their understanding remains narrow, and they strongly resist adopting new ways—true to their nature as Saidis. Fear rules their minds, keeping them shackled. Among the youth, many aspire to change, to learn about the world beyond their own. However, their motivation often lies in the pursuit of success, recognition, and, above all—money.

It remains a male-dominated world where women are treated as objects to be possessed and controlled. Love may flourish briefly, but the moment dominance takes hold, love withers, replaced by a bitter cycle of dependence. Thus, the daily gender battle plays out in most homes—an extreme polarization of the sexes, particularly in the Arab world, where gender roles are dictated more by societal constructs than by nature itself.

Men, deeply fearful of the feminine force—the power to create life, the strength of the soul—reduce women to mere vessels, existing to bear their children and serve their will. Women, in turn, conform to this expectation, bringing unnecessary suffering upon themselves. Female genital mutilation (FGM), though illegal, remains a widespread practice, with 75% of women still subjected to it.

As resistance to these constraints grows, frustration simmers beneath the surface, hidden behind the illusion of a happy family life—kullu tamam—while many long for a more fulfilling experience of love and existence.

A labyrinth of societal rules dictates behavior, stifling authenticity. In the effort to conform, people craft facades that suffocate their senses, repress creativity, and twist their very spines into submission. They strive to be "good," to comply with corrupt standards, hoping for a smooth, secure life and the safety of their families. But in doing so, they become opportunists—each one scrambling to protect their own interests.

Coherence? Lost.

I have the gift of a keen and highly developed sense of perception. While I am generalizing here—acknowledging that exceptions always exist—these are the most glaring issues at hand.

Egyptians remain a largely unified people through their shared ways of living. However, their collective self-image is generally low and negative. They strongly resist change, bound tightly within the constraints of their communal mindset. There is much lamenting, yet little action—no one wants to take the first step toward meaningful progress. A significant part of this stagnation stems from the deep-rooted gender imbalance. Awareness is only beginning to emerge. Women of Egypt, wake up!

To the Truth Regarding Gender Relation:

Goddess Suckling Pharao!

I believe that for both myself and the Saidis, life and work in the fields—in nature—remain an unrecognized source of renewal. Though they see it merely as a necessity and part of their daily existence, it quietly sustains them nonetheless.

In all their steadfast oriental complacency, the Saidis have yet to discover self-reflection. Instead, they are driven by numerous obscure forces—fear, greed, the need to belong, submission to authority, and a deep sense of disorientation. These forces compel them to act as they do, much like elsewhere in the world.

Egypt was in a state of lawlessness when Mubarak stepped up to replace the assassinated Anwar El Sadat some 30 to 35 years ago. Uncertainty ruled for too long. The army and police stole from the people, as did the politicians—just like elsewhere.

Egypt enjoys 360 days of sunshine, I dare say! And its people are just as radiant, despite the turmoil simmering beneath the surface. They cling to flimsy hopes, hold their breaths, lament their unspoken words, and endure it all—playing their own Egyptian games.

Oh, wonderful people of Egypt! You might yet rediscover the treasure beneath your feet and seek the light within. I love you for your joyous, playful merriment, behind which you artfully conceal the other side of the coin—even from yourselves. And I thank you for challenging me to fight for my full respect among you, as a woman alone—not just a pretty thing to be used, drained, and discarded with contempt. As you like to say, "Not all the fingers on the hand are alike!" I take pride in not falling prey to your many attempts to "marry" me. And thank you for accepting me among you, even if you label me the "mad woman" and remain somewhat suspicious of what kind of person I truly am.

I feel deeply privileged to live on such sacred ground, bathed in such luminous energy. Shukran!

In return, I will never get tired of sharing my sheer humanness with you—my joy, my pain, my anger, my understanding, my kindness. I know, and I sense, that you value me for simply being myself—unveiled, unmasked, uncloaked, naked, vulnerable, and true. Yes, I am mad enough to dare.

Living under one roof with the Belgian woman, I slowly became aware of the "game" between her and her young Egyptian husband. I realized that both of them had selfish, vested interests in this relationship—nothing to do with love. Individually, they were tolerable, but together, it was painful to watch the false charade playing out beneath all their saccharine words. She was completely oblivious to her own behavior, lost in her egoistic mindset, unable to see the role she was playing—or what he intended. The air grew thick with the unspoken tension of their deceit. Eventually, I could no longer bear the stench of it and dared to speak out. That made it clear—I had to leave.

But where to?

Ahmed invited me to live in his family home with him, his wife, and their children. He took me before his father, who welcomed me into their lives. However, to avoid gossip, I was told I would need to marry Ahmed. I made it clear: I would agree, but only on the condition that Ahmed would never ask me to consummate the marriage. Strange glances passed from father to mother to son and back again, but my terms were accepted without further debate. Said—done. The very next day, Mohammed, Ahmed's eldest brother, drafted the marriage contract, and it was finalized.

Ahmed Kenawy, My Handsome Young Paper "Husband"

I packed a few belongings and moved into the Khadi's house, sharing a flat with Ahmed, his wife, and their two children. His firstborn son, Jasr, just three years old, was a wild, radiant bundle of energy. We became instant friends—he awakened the wild child in me, the one I had never been allowed to be. His joy was infectious.

But my connection with him was not well received. After a while, his mother would drag him away, roughly snatching him up by the arm. Again and again, I witnessed the systematic destruction of his purity and innocence. His fresh energy, instead of being cherished as a gift to the family, was suppressed.

Worse still, I saw his grandfather's brutal violence against him—for no reason at all. My heart ached. I spoke to Ahmed about it, but he merely shrugged. "The father is the father," he said. "He cannot be questioned."

And so, the mindless cruelty continued.

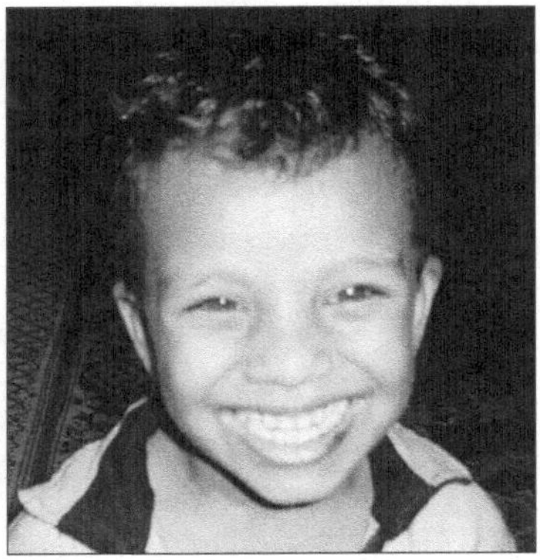

Ahmed's Son Jasr

Ahmed's second child was still a baby, but according to the grandmother, she was a "bad" child. She spoke those words with a look of utter disdain in her eyes. The cause, she explained, was a widespread practice in the region—intermarriage. Ahmed's wife was his direct cousin, chosen for him by his mother—the same woman now condemning the child as "bad." There was immense suffering and unhappiness in both parents because of this child. And soon, she returned to whence she came—she did not survive. This was the second child of theirs to meet the same fate.

I was deeply shocked to learn of this practice. Incest has been forbidden in ancient cultures worldwide for obvious reasons. It stunned me to see people living so close to nature yet still disconnected from its fundamental laws.

Life in the family upstairs was chaotic—hysterical, hectic, crazy, and messy. Out of kindness, Ahmed had insisted that I take the master bedroom, refusing any other arrangement. Meanwhile, his wife lived in a small bedroom with their children and husband. Ahmed showed her little regard beyond giving orders—telling her to iron his galabia if he planned to go out, cook his meals, prepare his tea, and so on. His only real responsibility was shopping, which we did together in his small car. We shopped generously and shared with the entire family.

During this time, I shared with Ahmed my extravagant dream—building a temple in Luxor, surrounded by a paradise garden, just as the ancients once did. First, I brought the design to life on paper. Then, we gathered the necessary materials and began constructing a three-dimensional paper model.

A Three Dimensional Paper Model

Ahmed was on fire now, and we had so much fun creating this model together, spinning more and more ideas. He took me to various domed buildings, inspiring us to build domes ourselves. Then, he showed me the land. I wanted it to be at the edge of the fruit fields, close to the mountains. So, we set out to negotiate with landowners, exploring different possibilities. But then came the pressing question—where would the money for this project come from? We calculated that we needed about 300,000 euros, including the cost of the land.

In May 2006, I boarded a plane to Germany, determined to find a generous sponsor for this ambitious project—a temple in Luxor, a city already boasting the largest number of temples in the world!

I remember returning to Luxor at the end of July. As I stepped off the plane, I was immediately engulfed by thick, boiling-hot, arid air. It must have been 50°C! Oh my! And yet, I had come back penniless, for all my efforts to find a sponsor had been in vain. Many doors had been slammed in my face. I was happy to be back but devastated to return with such bad news. Was this the end of our dream? Even this baby had to die! And then, another fear crept in—what about my home? Would they still allow me to stay despite having no money?

Well, they did. They could hardly throw me out just because I was broke. But I realized I could no longer afford to give away my healing hands for free—I needed to find a way to support myself. That was when I met a young woman in the process of setting up a hadana, a kindergarten, in Gezira village. We decided to collaborate, and I began crafting simple Montessori materials as learning tools for her children.

However, I was shocked by the way the small children were being taught. The teacher stood at the front of the class, a stick loosely in her hand, pointing at the blackboard, where the lesson was written. The stick danced back and forth as she chanted: Wahed, etneen, talata! The children, in unison, echoed her words: Wahed, etneen, talata! I quickly realized that before anything else, I would have to train the teachers—mostly young, unmarried girls who were uneducated and inexperienced. My friend, however, had been exposed to life in Europe. She had a keen, creative mind and progressive ideas, which gave me hope.

Meanwhile, life in the Khadis family house was becoming increasingly difficult to bear. I felt like I was losing myself. The purpose of our collaboration had collapsed, and I no longer felt welcome. I saw the looks on the women's faces—full of contempt—and I knew they gossiped about me endlessly, having little else to occupy their lives.

I must add here that Ahmed always respected my request not to touch me—honor to him for that. But to the women, a woman alone was unworthy. And one without children? Unthinkable.

The Hadana - Kindergarten

My new friend, Hamida, invited me to come and share a house with her. She lived in her brother's home—a modern house built with the help of his British wife, where nothing was lacking in terms of basic comfort.

And so, I accepted her invitation. The Khadi family was shocked. Hamida's family was nearly outcast in the village ever since her mother had thrown out her father for his habit of marrying a new wife every three moons. Eventually, she had enough. In an act of defiance, they tied him up and left him in the street. The thought of it made me chuckle—I admired their rebellious spirit. These were exactly the kind of strong-willed women I wanted to spend time with, even if it meant making enemies with Ahmed's family and the entire village.

I moved in with all my belongings, which had grown considerably—order, comfort, and perfection were important to me. Hamida and I spent countless hours together, exchanging ideas on how to improve the lives of children in Luxor.

The Team of the Hadana = Kindergarten

Children in the Hadana

Then, the conversation shifted to money. She needed funds for her project and, of course, expected me to contribute. When I told her I didn't have any to give, she refused to believe me and kept pressuring me.

One night, she suggested that I share her bed—what? I was shocked. I simply told her that I was not inclined that way and had no interest in sex. Again, she didn't believe me. Things were becoming more and more difficult. The foundation of our collaboration—our mutual understanding—had been badly damaged. I needed to go because the more I understood her psychological state, the more I sensed her suffering, along with her mother's.

In reality, she was seeing a cousin of hers who visited regularly and spent a great deal of time with her. But that was none of my concern. There was just too much confused energy. I knew I had to leave. But where to?

I had no memory of how I managed to finance myself at that time. Yet somehow, I was able to find a wonderful penthouse apartment on the fifth floor in Gezira, close to a canal that ran parallel to the Nile. The views were breathtaking, stretching in all directions. Most of all, I was relieved to have my life back to myself again. Up there, I could finally clear my tired mind from all the human messiness I had been entangled in. I rested and embraced the solitude.

Needy Women

By now, I had come to understand the common game played with female tourists who arrived without male company. I grasped it thoroughly, in all its details. Mature women were effectively trafficked into this dynamic, and upon arriving on the West Bank, one could observe the so-called "catching game." Young, handsome, elegant, and ever-so-charming boys—usually around twenty—would approach these women, engage them in flirtatious conversation, and soon disappear with them into a hotel. A perfect fit? This was how "happy marriages" were forged. The women experienced intense, passionate, and seemingly natural sex with a virile young man eager to prove his manhood—plus, he got paid for it. A dream? Perhaps. But ironically, while society often labeled these women as prostitutes, it was actually the young men selling their prowess for money.

Time and again, I encountered women who were addicted to these encounters, even as they were exploited and abused in every possible way. Were they foolish? No. They were simply starving for connection and fulfillment but did not know how to find it in a truly meaningful way. Instead, they became sex addicts, paying a high price for fleeting intimacy. One of them was Ingrid, a German woman of my age, utterly consumed by the kind of sex on offer there—no matter the circumstances. Though I never experienced it firsthand, I had an intuition about the nature of this game.

Ingrid was in love with an Omda, a prince—a dream of a man, perhaps. But upon waking? The reality was far from the fantasy. He had a long-standing relationship with a British woman who had built him a massive villa, in which he placed Ingrid as part of yet another tangled love affair—a catastrophic one. Disrupted minds, greed, and despair played out in self-destructive patterns on both sides. Through Ingrid, I found myself venturing to a remote village called Seoul, nestled at the desert's edge. There, he had yet another villa. How many European women did he use to fund his lifestyle? I had no idea. But what was I doing in the midst of all this madness?

Still playing the role of the helper, the healer, the lifesaver. And still, to no avail. Ingrid was so deeply entangled in this toxic web that she nearly took her own life. She was as trapped as so many others.

Ingrid loved animals. One day, someone brought her a young falcon with clipped wings. She took him into her flat. On a whim, I named him Fridolin, and whenever I visited her, we enjoyed his company.

Am I not an angel? Just had a bath!

I thank God that I had the sanity and self-respect to see through this game despite many attempts to pull me into it. Sorry, boys—I'm not on that market! I had already seen enough of this gender game with so-called "mature" European women. Having lived in Africa, I had encountered my fair share of polygamous men looking to exploit women. I was done with it—for good.

Even writing about this now fills me with reluctance because I spent far too much time immersed in it. It took me a while to understand that these women were not just victims—they were hooked. They craved the passion despite the pain it brought them. In German, the word for passion, Leidenschaft, literally means "that which creates suffering." And there it was. This pattern revealed a profound lack of self-worth, a deep-seated neediness, and an insatiable inner void. A neglected, abused, disrespected, unloved, and abandoned child existed on both sides of this gender game.

As a society, we have become disconnected from our natural gender roles and the complementary forces they represent. Their harmonious collaboration is the foundation of life—its continuation, growth, expansion, and evolution. Our current understanding of gender identity needs careful examination, as many distorted, ill-programmed beliefs have led us away from the true nature of gender relations and their higher potential.

I believe this is what eats away at the very root of all human problems in our world today. Gender relations form the smallest units of any community, society, or nation, serving as the entry portals for all unborn souls yet to arrive among us—each continuing their journey of learning and growth.

As I reflect on why I attract gender imbalance into my field, I realize that this issue is, of course, a significant part of my own journey as well. My feminine essence had been deeply wounded, suppressed, and denied, leading me to reject this aspect of my soul. I carried immense rage against the male gender because, in my eyes, men have long escaped accountability for countless atrocities while women are scrutinized relentlessly until some fault is found. Society blames women for everything that goes wrong. This injustice screams for change—STOOOOOPPPP!

As I ponder further, I recognize the need to reconcile the feminine and masculine aspects within my own soul—consciously and profoundly. I must integrate these energies, allowing them to find a natural balance within me to achieve wholeness.

This balance will empower me to be both gentle and strong, vulnerable and compassionate, understanding and forgiving, caring and accommodating, receptive, creative, and open-hearted. At the same time, I can be sexually and spiritually strong, authentic, active, and dynamic. I seek to be crystal-clear, courageous, protective, supportive, vigilant, open-minded, inventive, progressive, and strong—both physically and mentally. Above all, I aspire to be truly response-able.

At present, I feel that my masculine aspects are more dominant than my feminine ones, even though one of my teachers once told me that I have managed to maintain both qualities in equal measure. This suggests that there is untapped potential within me—potential that requires attention so I may fully align with my highest calling. And so, the work begins!

I am learning to release my rage, replacing it with understanding. I now see that men also suffer under the weight of gender imbalance. They, too, are burdened by the rigid roles and relentless pressures imposed upon them over the past 6,000+ years of male dominance. The very chains that bind women also bind men.

May this deepest aspect of our collective soul finally be healed!

May we all recognize the limitless power within us—beyond gender—and activate it for the benefit of all creation!

May we consciously and actively recreate ourselves in alignment with the grand unfolding of life, shaping it moment by moment, through us and by us.

Now, back to me: Through Ingrid, I found myself living in Seoul, the last village to the north on the West Bank that still belongs to Luxor. We often took long walks into the barren desert, inhaling the arid scent of rock and sand, feeling the dust carried by the wind, and enduring the merciless heat of SunRa. The vastness of the land, shaped endlessly by the elemental dance of wind, earth, and time, stood as a silent testament to nature's power and resilience.

Mohinder

One fine day, as I crossed the city on the ferry, I encountered a charismatic and magnetic personality. He sat down opposite me and immediately fixed his gaze upon me. He was striking—tall, with black hair and a dusky complexion. It was easy to tell he was of Indian origin, and he looked straight at me with a warm, unwavering smile. I smiled back, and just like that—BAM—the connection was established.

At the time, I was struggling financially. I was on my way to find a job at one of the large hotels in the area, hoping for any opportunity—help, support, advice—anything that could improve my situation.

Mohinder

To cut a long story short, I found myself entangled in a complicated three-way dynamic, though I had decided not to be romantically involved with Mohinder. It wasn't long before I realized he was heavily addicted—he drank, used drugs, anything he could get his hands on. He was trapped in a toxic relationship with a wealthy, drunken Scottish madame who treated him like a servant but kept him around because she had money to spare.

What on earth was I doing with these people? Were there any "normal" people left in the world? Why did I always end up surrounded by such chaos? "Good morning, sista, wake up!" But I didn't wake up—not yet. Even after a thousand such lessons, I failed to see what life was trying to show me. I still saw myself as a victim of circumstance, yet I endured it all with humor and an incredible inner strength. I carried my metaphorical toolbox everywhere, always trying to fix the suffering around me.

Through Mohinder, I found accommodation at a hotel just around the corner from where he lived with the madame. The hotel belonged to Mohamed, a kind and caring man. We spent many nights together—talking, laughing, and enjoying each other's company. We frequented our favorite fish restaurant, engaging in the same old, superficial small talk I had grown used to at my parents' home. But what I truly cherished were the moments of quiet companionship—eating together from the same plate, sitting in silence around the fire on biting cold winter nights. Mohamed, a Cancerian like my father, had an unspoken understanding that comforted me.

Before long, I became part of the family, feeling safe and a sense of belonging—until Mohamed's business-savvy wife arrived from Norway with a group of wealthy guests. I had to leave. She would have been suspicious of me, even though there was nothing going on between Mohamed and me.

That's not entirely true! We did have a beautiful rooftop-hug story. Many nights, we sat on the roof of his hotel late into the night when no one was around. Under the stars, we shared food and held each other tightly—very tightly. And little by little, we kissed, and then, well… this and that. I was very clear about not taking things further, but I truly cherished those embraces under the moonlit sky, listening to the distant sounds of animals, scattered voices, and someone playing the oud.

He was a quiet man with a kind of style that resonated with me. And those hugs—those hugs had something in them! That's all I needed. I savored those stolen hours, that sweet, fleeting intimacy with a stranger—for a stranger he remained. We did not talk much, but there was depth in him, a certain poetry I could sense, though he was bound by his Saidi ways. It was a sweet memory.

He once spoke of hiding me away in some far-off desert village until he had taken care of his three sons—males, ya habibi. But I have a head to think, a heart to feel, and I do what I like—what serves me!

And so, where to next? Thanks to Providence, I found a "buffalo" house in Seoul for a modest rent. It was a simple, unfinished place, and oh, how I dreaded moving in. But when the time came and I finally settled in, I realized—I was free. Free to live my life again. What I thought would be a miserable time in that dreaded buffalo house turned out to be one of the most precious periods of solitude—a quiet victory. And, in time, I turned it into my own little palace.

The Buffalo House/House of Nasr

After three months in the buffalo house, I met Nasr from Raoaga. He was Mohinder's immediate neighbor, the owner of a massive four-story house which remained empty because he lived and worked in Switzerland. He offered me a freshly finished flat on the third floor, and I moved in with my belongings. On the second floor was the spacious apartment belonging to Swiss Eva and her husband. They entrusted me with its care, ensuring it was ready whenever they or their friends came to visit.

I was now the housekeeper of this villa—wow. Ouf, Nasr's younger brother, visited me regularly. I loved him; he was sweet and innocent, knowing little about the world beyond the one he had grown up in. My love for him was purely that of a brother.

My circle of "friends" now consisted mainly of men—no more women trapped in their passions. I quietly attended the nightly gatherings of men, though I did not understand enough Arabic to fully participate in their conversations. This gave me time to retreat inward, yet I was still wrapped in their company. Since there were many of them, I felt safe. For me, it was a quiet time. I sat silently for hours, for days and nights, just existing. Passive. Yet—not entirely independent.

I had no trouble renewing my visa; I simply crossed over to the tourist police office on the Eastbank once a year and paid a small fee. But again, I needed an income to stand completely on my own feet.

Ouf

So I searched, and, lo and behold, I found work at the Jollieville Moevenpick Hotel, located on an island in the Nile, surrounded by a beautiful park with ancient trees and vibrant bird and plant life. The hotel consisted of multiple pavilions and had a huge pool, offering breathtaking views of the mountain ranges on the Westbank.

I secured two jobs there: one as a massage therapist—an additional service for guests, alongside a British woman who had actually helped me get the position—and another as the manager of the hotel's small childcare center, where parents could leave their children to enjoy some free time. I also offered yoga classes in the garden. The pay was not much, but it was better than nothing. As always, when fate turns in my favor, I embrace my work with enthusiasm.

The carefree days were soon over. I worked six days a week, around ten hours a day. But I loved the setting and made the best of it—also in my nature. Every day, I crossed the Nile and took either a local microbus taxi or the Jollieville transport to the hotel. This expanded my understanding of life there and exposed me to the internal politics of a large business like Jollieville. The British woman who had helped me secure the job confided in me often, sharing her frustrations and complaints about what went on behind closed doors.

I did my work as best as I could, starting each morning with a headstand in the parklike landscape, hoping guests might join me for yoga—not many did. I poured my energy into the children's play center alongside my young Egyptian assistant and gave my special relaxing and healing massages to grateful guests.

One day, a guest had originally booked a massage with the British lady, but upon seeing me, she canceled her appointment and asked for my services instead. That was when things took a turn for the worse. Soon after, I was summoned to the GM's office, only to be told that I was no longer needed. WHAAAT? After all my effort and hard work?

On my way home, I cried bitterly. The same British lady who had gotten me the job was now responsible for my dismissal.

Still, I tried to make the best of the situation—I could finally relax and enjoy some time for myself. But, of course, money quickly ran out. Once again, Mohamed came to my rescue. He introduced me to his cousin, who crafted reliefs from plaster of paris, featuring pharaonic images. He wanted me to paint them, to bring them to life with color.

The Weighing of the Heart

The pay was minimal, but I found joy in sitting on Eva's terrace, overlooking the fields around Raoaga, listening to music, and carefully painting the ancient images. These reliefs depicted scenes of daily life from the past—Gods and Goddesses, Pharaohs and their Queens, and the timeless principles of existence, subjects I had studied intensely years ago in Berlin. In that quiet space, I found both survival and enjoyment.

Additionally, I offered my massage services locally. The men were eager for them, but they were unwilling to pay fairly, and there was always an uncomfortable undercurrent of sexual tension. Many of them carried a foolish pride in their so-called prowess—something I had absolutely no interest in. Eventually, I decided to abandon this source of income.

It soon became clear that this job was not providing enough financial stability, so I continued my search.

Thanks to Mohamed's active intervention once again, I was invited to join a ride on the famous Dahabeya—a large sailboat designed in the traditional style of the old days. It was a stunning, stately vessel furnished to the highest level of luxury. I was accompanied by one of the company's owners, who offered Dahabeya trips up the Nile to Aswan, along with his crew of about twelve young men and a couple from Paris, who were the only guests. Enrike, from Mexico City, wanted to see if I would be a good fit to work on a sailboat like this one. He invited me to travel with them to Esna, board the Dahabeya there, and later return to Luxor from Edfu. This meant I could stay on the boat for two full days and nights. How incredibly lucky I was!

Dahabeya

She was breath-taking—pure white throughout, with luxurious beds fitted with the finest mattresses, making it feel like sleeping on a cloud. Every detail exuded supreme quality and impeccable cleanliness, chosen with exquisite taste. It was a true jewel. If I remember correctly, it could accommodate up to

24 guests, but thankfully, there were only four of us. The crew remained mostly in the background, quietly tending to their tasks—from cooking to adjusting the sails and everything in between.

As we boarded, I had to pinch myself. Was this even real? We checked into our rooms, and I was awestruck—what a massive bed dressed in the finest snow-white cotton sheets! As we set sail and began gliding gently across the water, I felt an overwhelming sense of gratitude for the privilege of being there—an experience for which guests paid 1,000 euros for a week.

Sitting on the deck, we watched the ancient pharaonic landscape drift by in slow motion, perfectly in tune with the silence. There was no intrusive motor noise to shatter the timeless tranquility of the arid desert bordering the river, with its thin strip of fertile land on either side. Time seemed to dissolve into eternity as we floated along the smooth surface. In certain places, the landscape reflected perfectly on the water, leaving the mind speechless in awe. My breath deepened, my body relaxed completely, and we all surrendered to the simple bliss of just being.

The four of us thoroughly enjoyed delicious meals together on the deck, savoring both the food and each other's company. Here, silence transformed into inspiring conversations and fascinating discussions about the Pharaonic past. At one point, Enrike pulled me aside to discuss what would be expected of me if I wished to work with them. To my surprise, the role was not demanding in the conventional sense of work as I knew it. My main responsibility would be to ensure that all guests felt content and harmonized. I would subtly manage seating arrangements during meals and create a seamless, enjoyable experience for high-paying guests with lofty expectations.

Oh my God! Diplomacy has never been my strong suit. The salary seemed rather modest, though the job did come with full board and lodging.

I also provided massages for the couple on board, and they thoroughly enjoyed them. I still laugh at the memory of maneuvering across the massive mattress, trying to reach every part of their bodies.

I cherished every moment of this unique experience with all my senses. But eventually, my time on the boat came to an end. After two truly blissful days and nights on the beautiful Dahabeya, I stepped back onto solid ground. Gratefully, I bid farewell to everyone and took a taxi back to Luxor. Only then did I fully realize the profound impact of this trip—the cleansing, soothing, and healing effect it had on me. I had been gliding through heaven. Bliss and gratitude filled my heart.

However, I knew this job was not for me, and Enrike seemed to agree. After observing me closely, he concluded that I was not suited for life on board.

A strange mix of relief and despair washed over me. My purse was painfully empty. With nowhere else to turn, I decided to have a word with God. Lying on my bed, I made a dramatic declaration: if God couldn't take better care of His child than this, then she might as well die. I was completely fed up and saw no way out. This was serious—I meant it!

As I lay there, ready to surrender, tears streamed down my face. Oh my God, how I pitied myself! My inner witness couldn't help but chuckle at the theatrical scene I was creating. And then, just as my despair peaked, the telephone rang.

It was my neighbor, Mohinder.

"What's wrong?" he asked. "I feel you're not okay."

Hearing me sob, he came over without hesitation. He sat beside me, listened to my woes, held my hand, and then—bless his kind soul—handed me 50 EGP for my empty purse. Tears dried, death forgotten, life moved on! Hahahaha!

Two weeks later, the wonderful couple from Paris returned to Luxor and checked into the exquisite five-star luxury hotel, El Moudira. Nestled on the West Bank at the edge of the desert, this stunning hotel was built in the style of a traditional Moroccan palace by a vibrant Lebanese woman. The couple, kind as ever, spread the word about the quality of my massages. And as fate would have it, Madame Zeina, the hotel's owner, was in desperate need of an additional massage therapist!

After a successful test massage, I was hired on the spot—with excellent pay. What a day to celebrate!

I felt as if I could take off from sheer joy. How quickly moods can shift! We humans are truly remarkable creatures.

With this newfound job, my life took a profound turn. Each day, I traveled by hired taxi from Raoaga to a location well beyond Medinet Habu. After months of reclaiming my life, I realized my time in Raoaga was coming to an end. It was time to fulfill my dream of living along Memnon Road, where the Colossi of Memnon still stand proudly today.

I had already set my sights on a house long before. It belonged to Hagag, whose younger brother, Sayyed, I had met during my first days in Gezira, Luxor. Sayyed ran a shop selling Galabiyas, mostly catering to tourists. When Hagag showed me the house, I chose the flat I wanted. We agreed on the rent, and before long, moving day arrived.

To my own surprise, I had accumulated far more belongings than I expected over the past two and a half years of struggle. As my things were loaded onto a truck, I waved goodbye to Ouf, Raoaga, and all the "friends" I had made there.

It felt liberating—truly liberating! I was the queen of my life once again. I still maintained some connections in Raoaga for a while and held onto my two trusted drivers—each as different as day and night.

Life along the Memnon Road

It was now September 2008, and I found myself returning once again. Apart from my wonderful trips to work—which I cherished for the fun moments shared with my drivers and the breathtaking scenery—I was captivated by the beauty that surrounded our journey. We traveled through landscapes adorned with fiery acacia in full bloom and thick clusters of multicolored bougainvillea lining the streets on either side. In the distance, the beloved mountain range stood tall, with the pyramid-shaped Qurn rising majestically. Our route took us along the canal, past vast fields where sugarcane swayed gracefully in the breeze, and stately maize stood in orderly rows. No matter how many times I had made this journey, I never ceased to love it.

I also adored my time at work, set in an elegant location where beauty meets the eye at every turn. Nestled within a vast, lush garden, the surroundings were a masterpiece of art and design. The villas, which hosted guests from all corners of the world, were adorned with stunning décor and artwork.

View of the Reception and Boutique Area from the Garden

Every detail in the hotel reflected exquisite creative taste. From the harmonious blend of colors and floral designs to the handcrafted clay vessels, wooden mirrors, and intricately carved mushrabiya woodwork, every element contributed to a symphony of beauty. A fountain, adorned with turquoise floral tiles, stood as a centerpiece, while patchwork-style pathways wove through the grounds. Everywhere I looked, there was a seamless harmony—a feast for the senses that left an everlasting impression.

Ever so Inviting: Dinner in the Courtyard behind the Reception

The massage villa was near the grand swimming pool, and during summer, I spent many nights swimming alone under the starry sky, waiting for my driver to pick me up after work. I met such wonderful people there as guests. This job was a blessing in many ways—I overcame my reservations about wealthy people and discovered that they could be kind, humble, and beautiful inside. I was thrilled to be in such high demand and to receive generous tips, which I sometimes shared with my drivers when I felt like it.

Al Moudira Pool Area

I also cherished my alone time at home, choosing to meet friends for quality time together. One of the most meaningful connections I formed was with Leela, an elderly Indian woman who had lived in the U.S. for many years. Our conversations were deeply inspiring, as she was on her spiritual journey just as I was on mine. What initially brought us together was our shared fascination with Pharaonic Egypt—its monuments, history, and profoundly spiritual way of life. She became a special highlight of my journey. Over the years, she had struggled with physical weakness and illness, and her time eventually came to pass on when life took us to different continents.

I opened my home to host meditation meetings with women and found myself marveling at the illustrious beings who had once landed on the silty shores of the Nile there in Luxor. One day, we had the rare opportunity to meditate inside a cave adjacent to a family home up in the mountains. The cave was entirely empty—no inscriptions, no markings, just a void in the belly of the mountain where we were almost entirely cut off from sound and light. It offered us a profoundly different experience.

I thoroughly enjoyed this carefree and fulfilling time, savoring the silent hours spent on the vast terrace overlooking the fields stretching endlessly in front of the house. To the left, they extended all the way to the base of the mountain range, while around the house, palm trees stood heavy with ripening dates. At dawn, I was thrilled to hear the wild cries of a falcon as it circled high above, and later in the morning, I was charmed by the sweet, rhythmic cou-cou-cou-cou-couuu of the hoopoe bird. Witnessing the cycles of nature throughout the year, I became increasingly attuned to their signs.

For instance, the shifting air signaled the arrival of dawn and dusk—each transition heralded by a subtle, cool suction in the atmosphere and a broad spectrum of rainbow hues unfolding along the horizon. At sunset, sparrows would rush to the persea trees with a tremendous commotion as if announcing the close of day. I adored the wild games of the swallows at dusk—their daring, playful dives as they joined and parted, then joined again, gracefully clearing the skies of insects with each surge through the air. The ever-present krakras of crows added their own commentary as if they had something of utmost importance to contribute.

In the mornings, the most soothing sound was the gentle cooing of pigeons, ushering in the fresh new day with their peaceful, tender melodies.

Occasionally, a lovesick donkey would make its predicament unmistakably known, its bray loud and desperate, its manhood on full display—eliciting broad, foolish grins from the men nearby. And, of course, the village dogs had their moments of collective madness, usually choosing the quietest nights to engage in their raucous yaff-yaff-yaff, much to the annoyance of many.

One of the most touching sights I observed was three generations working together in the fields, with the additional help of two oxen yoked together, slowly raking through the thick, fertile soil under the guidance of the son. Behind them, the grandfather sowed the seeds into the freshly opened earth while a donkey, pulling a wooden rod, followed behind to cover the seeds with soil. To add weight, the grandson stood on the rod, ensuring the seeds were properly buried. This image stirred something deep within me—it was so ancient, so connected to nature, a timeless collaboration with Mother Earth and a seamless continuum of generations bound together.

This happened just outside my home. I felt incredibly blessed to live in such a world, surrounded by cows, buffalo, turkeys, and ducks—my neighbors—each entertaining me with their unique music. In the distance, ancient monumental temples, tombs, and an impressive mountain range stretched north and south, completing the breath-taking scene.

As I write, I realize this was a truly special time in my life—a time of deep reconciliation, comfort, and healing for my soul. I shared my days with the Saidis, those simple, unassuming people, so unaware of their own essence that they seemed almost innocent. They embraced their fate with boundless merriment and laughter. I cherished my time there, grateful for every experience—the trials and joys, the relentless tests of my patience, and the gradual expansion of my heart, opening ever more with each passing day. Their generous hospitality was interwoven with subtle, cunning attempts to ensnare me in their familial web—not merely to be milked for favors, but also to be cared for. Yet, by some grace of my soul, I had no real need of such care.

As I reflect, countless moments come to mind—perhaps small, insignificant to anyone else, yet collectively forming the intricate tapestry of my life. After all, is it not these little, unexpected but deeply real moments that weave the web of our existence?

The Egyptian summer was scorching, the heat relentless in the late afternoon. When the shade stretched across the rooftop, I would retreat there, escaping the confines of my flat and the whirring fan, seeking open air—even if it was still stifling. Sitting in the shade of the palm trees, now heavy with ripe clusters of dates, I overlooked the fields stretching north toward Qurna town. To the west, the mountain range unfolded before me—the temple of Hatshepsut, the tombs of Asasif and the Nobles, the Ramesseum, the German House, and behind it all, the Qurn, its peak towering above the Valley of the Kings, all seemingly within arm's reach.

I searched the sky for divine messages hidden in fleeting cloud formations. I observed the ever-changing rhythm of the fields—the grazing donkeys, their masters lost within the sugarcane, pulling weeds or squatting in the alfalfa fields, cutting the very fodder their animals would later feast on. Some waded through the irrigation channels, clad in snow-white undergarments, surrounded by flocks of egrets—their ancient companions—as they orchestrated the water's flow, just as their ancestors had done for thousands of years.

I watched enormous bundles of grass with legs moving through the fields—families tending their herds of sheep, seeking shade and respite in the cooling evening breeze as the sun, like Sun Ra himself, sank low on the horizon. A donkey, seized by a sudden longing for freedom, bolted from its master, galloping wildly before being chased down, mounted, and reminded—through firm but familiar blows—who truly held the reins.

The wind bent the palms, their long fronds shimmering in the golden light.

And one day, I saw a dozen storks standing in the field right in front of my house.

And on a Muslim Saturday, I saw the youth dressed in their finest—it was wedding night, which meant party night! With deafening noise and reckless speed-racing along Memnon Road, they unleashed their untamed energy, a wild display of unguided youthful exuberance. Hullaballoo.

The lights on the mountain flickered to life, but the sky bore little of its usual celestial artwork that night. Still, I had often witnessed astonishing messages written in that ever-mystical, radiant glow after Ra had

descended into the netherworld.

I listened to the voices of the animals—their cryptic yet, at times, strikingly clear chatter. Moh, baeh, kikeriki… ihaihaiha… The wind rustled through the leaves while birds filled the air with their endless quarrels and love songs.

I savored the majestic sight of Horus, the falcon, soaring effortlessly higher and higher, gliding in deliberate, languid circles, as if for the sheer joy of it. Oh, what a King of the Skies he was!

I watched as the light of Ra tenderly kissed the southern face of the mountains, illuminating them with a golden glow. The feathery brushstrokes in the sky were delicate now, revealing layered currents of air swirling in their graceful goodnight dance for Ra.

Swallows swooped and dived, feasting on insects in midair with fearless precision.

K…k…k…k…k… A man passed by on his donkey, making his way home.

That night, Ra himself seemed to be the artist—his masterpiece painted across the sky. Angelic wings, open and vast; see for yourself in the picture attached.

The herds were driven home, their day's harvest of fodder loaded onto carts and transported to its final destination.

A chubby young boy galloped past on his donkey, shouting jippijeh in sheer delight, his legs swinging back and forth as if to propel the donkey forward with his own momentum. Nearby, a lone stork soared gracefully in slow, deliberate circles; its wings stretched wide before descending into a lush green field to join its kin.

To the southeast, the three towering mountain peaks still shimmered in Ra's fading light, standing in distant, silent splendor. That night, Ra seemed to have forgotten his colors, yet I adored his final glow. It lingered, potent and mysterious, with a quiet, almost mystical force.

As the light faded, the sounds of traffic softened, giving way to the hushed murmurs of the wind, distant voices, and the tender hues of the sky—so sweet, so delicate. Crickets chirped. Stars emerged. And the deeper Ra sank, the brighter the heavens blazed with their celestial fire.

The muezzin called. Mosquitoes began their nightly hunt. AM I NOT EVER SO BLESSED? There is so much more to tell. I explored Egypt from north to south, from west to east. I traveled to Aswan and Abu Simbel, Abydos and Dendera, passing through the western desert oases and the enchanting Siwa.

Assuan –The Pearl of the Nubian South – She Is a beauty

The glorious light of Sun Ra was a constant companion, and the ancient energy of this land was tangible everywhere. The lush greenery of the fertile lands along the Nile contrasts beautifully with the ever-changing desert—its shifting colors, moods, and forms never cease to captivate me. Traveling through Egypt was a joy. I cherished its unhurried pace of life, the arid heat, the meditative rhythm of existence, and the effortless way everything always seemed mumkin—possible. The desert held a magic I can neither fully describe nor explain, but I felt it deeply. I loved it—the vast, open expanses.

For six nights, I camped in the White Desert with my dear sister Maya. When it was time to return to "civilized life," we burst into tears. In the desert, life reveals itself in its purest form—immediate, raw, and profound. The silence is not empty; it is full of invitation, urging you to listen within, to meet your truest self. This is the desert's gift to those who are open to it—pure bliss.

The slow rhythm of life there makes it easier to live fully in the present moment.

It's hard to choose which images to share—I have so many!

The King's Valley

The Great Sand Sea around Siwa Oasis

My Neighbours in the Buffalo House in Seoul

Fellahin Family in Their Field – Acquaintance with the Land

Enjoying the Hot Spring in Siwa Oasis

Donkey Love and Then off to Meditate in the Temple with Aisha, My Sista

Siwa's Famous Shali, the Old Village Damaged by Heavy Rains

I will savor every moment of this for as long as it lasts, as all signs point to massive changes ahead. Yet for now, the sky burns in shades of crimson and pink—Ya Allah, what glory! Al Hamdulillah.

Who Paints Such Sweetness?

Another Kind of Sweetness in Abundance, Created by SunRa

My heart truly felt at home on Luxor's West Bank. But as time passed, the economy began to decline, and I could see the day approaching when I would no longer be able to sustain my wonderful life there. I also felt a sense of stagnation in my soul's journey. So, I made the difficult decision to let go of everything—giving up my flat and job, selling my belongings, gathering what money I had, and crossing the Atlantic to sit by the Pacífico, watching whales and dolphins.

It was December 2009, and I was 60 years old. That sounds much older than I actually feel!

Magic Moments of Dawn

Moonlit night – silence deep – all in sleep...
Subtly, gently, the night surrenders to the day's embrace,
As the Great Light beams out His radiance from deep down
The eastern horizon, announcing His advent...
The horizon dons sweet rainbow colours all around –
The stage is set – the King returns in triumph again.
The eastern skies alight in a pink-orange glow.
The heavy heat of night clears at once by a mighty suction of air –
Creation holds its breath – and here He comes:
His radiant glory shines from deep within on this day –
In dignity, He ascends,
A clear golden sphere, gently tinting all with His golden glow.
The birds jubilate, praising, and start their day's dues.
This day holds the promise of a sparkling light, like a diamond,
And a moderate heat, with a gentle breeze swaying the palms to and fro.
The mountain's aglow – Ra's light reveals its profiles as crystal clear –
This mountain beams with a light of its own...
All Ra's alchemy secrets are enclosed in its heart,
And Horus, the Enlightened One, circles above...
Oh, ancient Pharaonic ancestors,
Set your fire ablaze within me, I bid, once more.

There is so much more to share and discover. Once again, I extend my deepest gratitude to the ancient, sacred land of light for its generous hospitality and the abundance of beauty it has bestowed upon me.

I am also grateful for the eyes to witness its splendor, the ears to receive its whispers, the mouth to savor its gifts, and the soul to appreciate the countless riches of this blessed land.

Goddess Ma'at Representing Eternal Cosmic Order and Law

Homage to My Late Mother

She died on 21.12.08 at 4 a.m.
She is dead—left this world
To roam the Duat.
May her journey be guarded and blessed.
My mom went back home.
Myriads of emotions erupt inside me.
All my childhood drama comes up, so I see
The path which I took to finally be free.
I see, I see—
So clearly,
I see.
'Twas all in the mind,
This prison around me.
And the mind—now my tool—
To at last set me free.
I can now discard the most adamant beliefs.
They may leave along with her,
Lose their stronghold on me.
I cast off my weary shoulders
Much leaden weight along the road.
I've come a long, lonesome way,
Feel it's time now to arrive,
To go home alive.
As a bright, bright star in the darkest worldly night,
To shine my divine light as a torch for my kind.
I am blessed—ever so blessed.
I render thanks for my weary road
And share the jewels with those who seek.

Luxor, January 2009

EGYPT - MEXICO
The Bars of Imprisonment

In 2009, I successfully secured a wonderful job and a comfortable, charming flat in my favorite spot in Luxor, Egypt—on the west bank of the Nile. It was in close proximity to the Colossi of Memnon and major temples and tombs from ancient Pharaonic times, all within walking distance.

As the economy plunged into crisis, I found myself wondering—was this the right time to leave? Taking stock of my life, I realized there were other reasons why I might prefer to step away from this beloved land, at least for a while, despite the comfortable, settled life I had only recently acquired.

The second reason—one that cannot go unmentioned—is Egypt's unbearable heat from June through October. During this time, life shrinks into mere survival, where even breathing feels like hard work. Little else is inspired; the lucky ones spend their days indoors, under fans or air conditioning, while time drags on relentlessly.

Crossing the Nile into Luxor City feels like a form of capital punishment—one is drenched in sweat the moment they step outside. The dry, oppressive heat crushes every urge to move, think, or do anything at all. While some may thrive in such conditions, I am not one of them! I counted the weeks and days until October's end, struggling to endure that scorching inferno. Surely, there are other beautiful places in this world that do not impose such suffering on a European-born albino.

And then, of course, there was the eternal gender issue, which I have already recounted at length!

These reflections led me to the decision to leave this land, a place that had once made me declare upon my arrival: "I have come to live and die at the feet of El Qurn in Luxor, West Bank." The decision was made, and everything fell into place with remarkable ease and clarity.

I knew I would return one day to fulfill my pledge—but not alone. I intended to come back with a husband, or at the very least, a companion, someone akin to a personal bodyguard.

So, I turned to a website in search of a life partner, found a promising match, and arranged to meet him in Mexico—a land with a rich cultural heritage, stunning pyramidal structures, and the backdrop of Carlos Castaneda's legendary adventures. Its diverse flora, fauna, and indigenous traditions fascinated me, and above all, its moderate climate—with a pleasant average temperature of 25°C across much of its vast landscape—was a welcome change. Mexico, here I come!

I left Luxor on the freezing winter morning of December 15, 2009. Wrapped in my pink woollen coat, my breath turning to mist in the car, I sat beside Ahmed, my beloved driver. Silence bound us deeply. Over the years, through countless trips to and from my workplace and beyond, we had become good friends. Though we spoke different languages, our energies intertwined effortlessly, proving that the heart speaks a universal tongue.

At the airport, I unloaded my luggage, embraced Ahmed—along with all my winter garb—and departed in silence. And then, once again, I was alone on my journey through life while he returned to his own, bound within the embrace of his family and the confines of cultural and religious expectations.

My journey took me to Berlin via Cairo. Naturally, I chose a window seat, eager to savor one last view of that ancient, sacred land. From above, Egypt stretched beneath me like the floor of an ocean, its dry riverbeds forming intricate patterns in the sand and rock. I gazed upon the Red Sea—blue rather than red, of course—and then, as we neared Cairo, I spotted a dense, hazy cloud hanging over the city. Through the mist, minarets pierced the sky, their tips just visible. And then, in the distance, I saw them—hazy yet unmistakable—the pyramids of Giza. What a sight. What a heritage for humanity.

These monuments were not merely relics of the past; they were the legacy of Thoth, the ancient Atlantean, the eternal sage, the bringer of wisdom to humankind—a reminder of a glorious civilization lost in the depths of time.

Bye-bye Luxor Westbank and the Majestic Mountain Range

Berlin, a city that has experienced less of a glorious past in recent history but is steadily transforming into a magnetically attractive and dynamic hub in the West—drawing over a million tourists each year—was where my friend Donna awaited me. Together, we navigated the underground with my three large pieces of luggage, eventually arriving at her flat in Berlin Schöneberg, the heart of the city. This neighborhood is home to the legendary Rathaus, where, in 1961, J.F. Kennedy famously declared, "Ich bin ein Berliner!"

At Donna's place, I shared my space with Mui—an old, fat, and grumpy black cat—and countless spiders lurking in the corners. Their lives were strictly protected by Donna, an animal communicator. I was not particularly fond of having them so close to my bed and closet; they felt uncomfortably intimate for a city apartment. Still, I survived. I stayed for less than a month before traveling to Hamburg, where I spent three wonderfully intimate days with my old Papa. Then, on January 11, 2010, I boarded an Iberia flight bound for Madrid, Mexico City, and finally, Puerto Vallarta.

M e x i c o – Here I come!

I was truly excited about this new adventure, yet I had my reservations about whether the man I had chosen from the catalogue would turn out to be a good match. In our many telephone and Skype conversations, I could sense his expectations towering as high as Mt. Everest and a deep neediness—despite his claims of being an advanced spiritual adept.

I remained on guard, fully prepared to walk away if it was not right for me. But—I must admit—I had hopes (though, as Gangaji says, "Hopes are for children!"). At the same time, I sensed that this journey to the West—The Americas—was not going to be a carefree pleasure ride. This was about getting real at long last, at the age of 60!

What truly drew me to Mexico was an irresistible pull toward the ocean—the biggest one, please! The Pacific Ocean, that vast, endless body of water covering more than half the planet's surface. I longed to sit on its shores, commune with dolphins and whales, place my feet—my heart—my spirit—upon the ancient Motherland deep beneath its waves, and rekindle my memory of Her once more: Lemuria.

Looking back, I now realize that my journey was about reconnecting with the Sacred Feminine within. But to do so, I first had to face everything—the dark shadows lurking in the depths of my soul and, inevitably, all around me, reflected in the people I encountered and the world itself. I had spent a lifetime suppressing them, but the hour of truth had arrived, and avoidance was no longer an option. I was finally ready to end my internal suffering once and for all.

Allow me to elaborate on this part of my journey, for it is so fundamental to the human quest for self-discovery—the search for who I truly am.

As for the man I had chosen from the catalogue of potential life companions, it became painfully clear that we were utterly incompatible. After just two and a half weeks, I fled his tiny motor home and found a small apartment in San Pancho, the town he had brought me to after picking me up from Puerto Vallarta airport on January 13, 2010. From the moment we met, he treated me as though I were his possession, showing no genuine interest in me as a person—only as a much-needed addition to his deep-seated neediness and dysfunction. I sensed it almost immediately.

San Pancho

San Pancho (also known as San Francisco) is a charming little beach town just north of Bahía de Banderas on the west coast of this vast and wondrous country, Mexico.

I Landed Myself in Paradise!

After swiftly executing this separation—one that occurred without any natural bond having had a chance to form—two mighty, super-spiritual egos, weighed down by unresolved fears, went their separate ways. At last, I could breathe deeply and settle back into myself. Phew, that was close! I had cast him aside in utter disdain—what a fool he was! But then, the hour of truth came knocking hard on my door: nothing happens by chance.

This was a lesson, a reflection, a mirror held up to me. This was my choice, and it was a good one—a choice for myself to part ways with him. Yet, there are no coincidences in the people we meet. So, look! And as I gazed into the mirror of this encounter, I did see myself: the neediness, the desperate search for completion outside of me, the emotional grasping for love, for recognition, for someone to see and cherish me for who I truly am. I saw the hope for financial security through him—giving away my power yet again while simultaneously claiming to be an advanced spiritual seeker on the brink of enlightenment. Oh. My. God.

My Sweet Sista Mika, the Flying Yoga Teacher

I wanted to smash that mirror into a thousand pieces! But instead, I kept looking, embracing the truth of what I saw—even as I still fumed with anger at him. He kept lingering around San Pancho, poking his head in, hoping I had changed my mind. I was repulsed! I resisted every one of his attempts to talk, convinced it would lead nowhere worthwhile. I had shared such a small space with him, absorbed his entire energy field so fully that I was 150% certain: he was not for me.

I was furious with him—for everything that happened and everything that didn't. I was shocked to realize that we had no real way to communicate beyond superficial small talk. And that was certainly not why I had traveled thousands of miles across the globe. What was going on there? After all, I had co-created this bizarre experience. Yet, I had made it clear from the start that I needed time to get to know him before we became intimate partners.

I remember that I separated from my husband in 1979 for the very same reason: we could not communicate. No matter how hard we tried, we just couldn't talk things through. There was some level of energetic connection between us, but I could never truly share my thoughts with him.

With this man, however, the disconnect was even starker. What I felt from him energetically was the complete opposite of what he expressed verbally, and it shut me down completely. Was I supposed to call him out as a fraud? Hardly. The truth was, he had no depth. He was all mask—far more than I ever was. And I had no idea how to engage with him except by mirroring his behavior in a reversed way, unintentionally so. While he was always grinning from ear to ear, I found myself freezing my face into an increasingly stern and serious expression. Looking back, we must have appeared hilarious as a couple.

The more I reflect on this, the more I realize that this is a habit of mine that I need to change. Mirroring people's negative aspects only serves to create distance. It's like a child pointing and saying, "Look how stupid you are!" Mamma Mia, the games people play! Or rather, the games I play. That was my wall. I was resisting his shortcomings just as I was resisting my own. And in doing so, I had unknowingly trapped a lot of creative energy within myself. That needed to change.

Four months passed, and then I ran out of money. My efforts to find work or people who valued my art and healing work had mostly failed. What was the world showing me? Once again, I was penniless. My worth, it seemed, was ZERO—NIL—NOTHING. I was not worth a dime.

Gorgeous San Pancho Beachline – I Experienced hell in Paradise!

A tremendous fear surfaced. I slammed headfirst into the labyrinth of walls I had built around myself. And let me tell you, a labyrinth of thoughts can feel as solid as a city of brick walls. As those walls crumbled, I felt utterly lost—desperate beyond anything I had ever known. I begged for guidance and searched for help. But my so-called "spiritual" friends? They were full of the same empty, heartless advice that I had once been so quick to dispense to others, unasked.

Then, I stumbled upon a Codependents Anonymous group in San Pancho. I ran to their weekly meetings, and in that space, I finally found what I had been searching for: I am right here.

I had known about codependency. I had sensed my own codependent patterns long ago. I had understood that most people grow up in codependent family structures. And yet, I had once dismissed that path of self-inquiry—clearly because I hadn't been ready for the truth. But now? Now, I was.

Deep in the throes of crisis—the crisis of my life—I shattered into a million pieces. Shame washed over me for finally seeing the extent of my ignorant arrogance, hidden beneath layers of self-importance. Phew—it stank. How embarrassing. I felt twisted, fake, completely undone. Iiach.

I read every book they were willing to lend me. And then I knew, without a doubt: I WAS CODEPENDENT—completely, perfectly, with every possible ingredient contributing to the diagnosis. Oh MY GOD, again!

Shame flooded me as I realized how foolish I had been—thirty years of spiritual seeking and practice, yet I had been blind to this truth. Now, I had to face the reality of my own powerlessness and surrender to Mightier Hands, trusting they would pull me out of this chaotic predicament. I had to walk in truth and faith, even on an empty stomach, with utterly depleted financial, psychological, and spiritual resources. I had truly reached the end of my rope.

Now, I had to swallow my pride, relinquish control, and allow myself to receive help, support, and guidance from others.

The once-solid structure of my old self crumbled into fragments. The Glass Tower cracked beyond repair. My self-constructed psychic armor dissolved, revealing itself to be nothing but an illusion. And thank God, it was me who uncovered the truth at last!

It was also a blessing that I had done so much spiritual work and had a deep experience of Who I Am—otherwise, I might have completely fallen apart.

I changed my environment, retreating to a house in the jungle from June to the end of October. A generous Mexican friend offered to cover my food expenses—God bless her forever! I imposed a strict schedule on myself and meditated as much as possible. Desperation fueled my practice.

I found myself crying out to God—still picturing Him as something external, somewhere up above. That old, deeply ingrained program still had a hold on me. Yet, amidst the struggle, there were also moments of true bliss, silence, and peace.

My attachment to the ancient worlds of Africa and the Orient came up for inquiry. I had consciously chosen to move beyond patriarchal conditioning, to shift beyond those ancient programs and sink into the true root—SOURCE: Omniscient, Omnipresent, Omnipotent—the FEMININE.

The I AM—I am deathless, boundless, limitless Spirit. I am the Ever Free. I am the Eternal Present. I am Who I Am. This teaching from ancient Indian Yogic philosophy had been my meditation mantra for years. Yet, deep within my subconscious, another program still lingered, blocking my spiritual growth and awareness.

Then I found The Play of Consciousness by Swami Muktananda, founder of the Siddha Yoga organization. I devoured the book, reading it once, twice, again—working through it, resonating deeply. I sat in silence for hours, despite the oppressive heat and sweat, determined to conquer the restless monkey-mind and guide it, at last, to the abode of peace.

In that book, I found guidance. I found nourishment for my soul. And finally, I was able to fulfill what I had come into this life to do. I realized that my renunciation of material things—my strict, ascetic lifestyle—had been the wrong kind of renunciation all along.

The one thing I truly needed to renounce was the habit of seeing myself as separate—from the world, from others, from the Divine, the habit of compartmentalized thinking. It is liberating to realize that it is entirely possible to live a joyous, worldly life while remaining grounded in the deeper, eternal truth of Spirit—Omnipresent, Omniscient, and Omnipotent—not only within me but in all beings, in nature, in EarthMa and the Ocean, in the Planets and Stars, in every corner of Mother Nature and all of Her children. Living with this deep awareness—in harmony with all, in moderation, gently, peacefully, compassionately—we acknowledge that we are mere visitors on this beautiful Earth. We honor Her and Her generous gifts and strive to make the world a better place. Ultimately, we are here to recognize our own divine creative power.

The boiling, soaking, and thundering trials of the Mexican summer of 2010 came to an end. My hope of finding a way to support myself rose and fell—again and again. I was like a toddler learning to walk, spending more time on the ground than on my feet. I found myself slipping back into codependent behaviors, grasping for control over my life. Then came another turning point: I was asked to leave the house that had so generously sheltered me for months. It was another shock, another lesson in healing. But deep down, I knew it was time to move on. San Pancho was no longer the right place for me. With the kind intervention of a friend of a friend, I landed in Yelapa—to start anew.

Yelapa

I arrived in Yelapa on January 7, 2011, practically collapsing onto Playa Isabel, sinking into the sand with all my belongings. A few steps up a rickety, rocky trail led me to El Jardín, an eco-retreat. There, I was given a bed and food in exchange for four hours of daily work. My tasks included sweeping, keeping the space clean and orderly, doing laundry, and resetting the rooms for new guests—appearance, maintenance, and organization. I was, almost compulsively, good at this. Yet, the physical labor was more demanding than I had anticipated. My body ached, unaccustomed to such exertion.

In San Pancho, I had been living in concrete houses built for Gringos on holiday, designed to meet their standard level of comfort. Having lived in the pueblo, away from the sea, I spent most of my time indoors—either alone or in the company of distorted reflections of Westerners, with their crooked ways of thinking and living. Yes, I utterly and completely despised Western ways. I had successfully and deeply distanced myself from them, as though observing from outer space, in total detachment—or rather, separateness—analyzing their off-balanced ways critically and justifying my views by quoting Divine Law, as it was laid out in the beginning. It felt as if I had never been part of the Western world, nor did I ever feel that I was. It had always seemed strange to me—alien. And so, I clung even more fiercely to what I knew in the depths of my soul to be RIGHT.

This at least provided me with some sense of orientation amid the confusion and emotional insecurity of my childhood and youth. I repeatedly reminded myself that there was something to be wary of—something worth examining.

I always found an easy sense of recognition with people from ancient cultures, while Westerners seemed to shun, avoid, or even dislike me. And then, one day, I realized the truth: I, too, utterly disliked and wanted to avoid THEM.

Germans, generally speaking, are a species of their own. But here, in the "West," I was mostly surrounded by U.S. Americans and Canadians. They are typically free-spirited and open, connecting easily—chatting casually before flitting off, like butterflies, from one moment of fun to the next. They seem almost magnetically drawn to enjoyment. Their way of being might appear superficial, yet when I find myself alone with just one person, a deeper and more meaningful conversation is sometimes possible—occasionally even delightful. However, in groups, a different dynamic takes over. It becomes a fast-paced exchange of wit, a game of verbal ping-pong, where entertainment is the goal.

In such situations, I gradually adopted the role of a silent observer, watching my inner impulses—the old tendency to judge, the ingrained desire to play along and belong, and a newer, quieter instinct: to simply be present.

For I now live at El Jardin Garden Retreat, remember:

El Jardin Garden Retreat

At first, I believed they were out to kill me there. My body was neither accustomed to nor fit for all the clambering up and down those rickety, rocky trails, where every step required caution and balance. Hanging up the laundry, I often nearly tripped, sliding down the steep slope.

But as the weeks passed, I noticed my body growing stronger, gaining stability and a sense of well-being, though I remained vigilant with each step. Eventually, I regained my old elastic bounce—perhaps also fueled by an increasing joy for life in this gorgeous spot, nestled directly by the ocean, surrounded by an abundant, blooming tropical garden and forest.

Yelapa—a little pueblo with NO CARS, where only people and mules moved! The casitas at El Jardín, along with other rentals and private homes, were mostly palapa-roofed structures with open windows and walls that only rose halfway, allowing the ocean air to flow freely. Along with it came birds, butterflies, and other winged and four-legged visitors. There was no sense of enclosure—nature itself became a part of daily life.

I experienced profound healing in this environment; it nurtured my body, mind, emotions, and spirit. Nature is the impeccable teacher, the great mirror reflecting the many facets of our own being—the Supreme Healer! And I feel deeply nourished as a part of her.

Now, my challenge is summer's mighty thunderstorms, with their torrents of water falling all at once. When thunder shakes the mountain where I live, lightning blinds even my closed eyes, and the rain fuels an explosion of new life in the surrounding bush. Once the storm rages and retreats, an abundance of beauty unfolds before my eyes.

And then, with a deafening sound, the grand crickets announce a new inferno—how will this night unfold? Last night, the rain paid me a visit in my bed, and the wind sent the shutters flying, delivering its urgent message. Leo moon waxing, Mercury in retrograde—August 2011. A time to look within, face my fears, surrender to the Mighty Will, and remember: I am immortal. Deep breathing carries me through the stress in my gut during this Zeussian trial, as I trust that the Eternal Mother will see me through.

There is still much to learn at El Jardín, so many things. The ocean, in all her power, may one day decide to rise from her grand bed and climb the few yards to tickle my feet. Her mighty roar stirs both awe and fear as I observe Grandmother Luna pulling up Yemayá with the approaching full moon, flooding the rocky path once again. And so, I feel and perceive the intimate relationship between Luna and Yemayá.

Those Hanging Beds in El Jardin – GREAT to Sleep in!!!

Living in an open space with no protection from the elements was a challenge during the winter of 2011, from January to March. The cold nights meant wearing multiple layers and sleeping under four thick blankets—daring not even to poke my nose out. I quickly got used to using a pee bucket—no shivering through the gardens in the dead of night to expose my body to the freezing air.

Yet, all of this was nothing compared to the challenge of being the "sweepy" and dealing with so many spoiled visiting guests from the U.S. and Canada, with the occasional European in between. I met many sweet and interesting people—appreciative, positive, and respectful—but I also witnessed things that stung my eyes and revolted my mind, reinforcing my deep dislike for the ignorant arrogance of certain Westerners. Mirror, mirror… and a lot of anger surfaced time and again—

until I caught myself, stepped back, and let go. Perhaps that was where my anger finally dissipated.

When it came to the owners of EJ, I often slipped back into codependency, meaning I took on excessive responsibility multiple times—only to catch myself again. Thankfully, there was more tolerance for shortcomings than I was willing to extend, and through that, I learned to tolerate and accommodate dysfunctional behavior. Humanness! My heart began to relax, my mind softened, and I started curbing my habit of taking on others' burdens. Slowly, I set clear, appropriate boundaries. I had begun walking the path to my Authentic Self, and with each gentle step, I felt so much better.

A few days after arriving in Yelapa, I mentioned to my new German friend, Angelika, that I might want to share my life with a companion—to finally master this chapter of my life. Lo and behold, she arranged a meeting with a long-standing friend who had the same wish. She even tried to throw us onto her swing bed together at our first encounter! So, we dated—there was attraction and flow—but I ignored all the red flags flashing before me. Before long, I became physically involved with him, something I had never done so quickly before.

We shared some wonderfully creative hours, though our nights together were far from fulfilling. Do men only know that old rabbit routine? Still, I gained insights from the experience. Then, inevitably, disillusionment struck. Just as quickly as infatuation had taken over, I was jolted out of my trance. I had to ask myself: WHY am I STILL attracting the SAME type of dysfunctional man into my life? Alarm bells rang—I needed to look deeper and stop blaming "the men." Enough with the victim mindset!

And with that, I was done seeking a companion. Hadn't my life always been simpler and more peaceful without one? After ten years of living a free, content, celibate life, I should have known better. Yet, traces of codependency resurfaced. But with each relapse, I became better at recognizing and curbing this ingrained tendency. This painful but necessary shock propelled me toward truth—all the way. It was time to illuminate every blind spot, to reflect with absolute honesty. No more hiding, no more self-deception. It was time to uncover WHO I AM, a truth I had glimpsed many times but never fully embraced.

It was time to grow up and take full responsibility for my thoughts, feelings, and actions. No more holding on, holding back, or keeping parts of myself obscured. I had to bring everything into the light, allowing my energy to finally serve a higher purpose. No longer would I live as a victim, trapped in a stagnant existence, as my mother had. My inner self was desperate to be respected, to be free. Why had it taken me so long to reconnect with that truth? I had detached from life, from my own inner energy—lost in the maze of my mind. Despite my deep longing to be my true self, I remained stuck in ignorance.

But life is flawless in its lessons. Perhaps I would never understand why things unfolded as they did. So, I let go. At last, I DID THE WORK. I stopped. I investigated. I inquired into my habitual wiring and went beyond—into the deep, still pond of I AM. Ah—home. I breathed. Expanded. Felt the fullness, the joy, the peace. Home. Always there, waiting for me to return.

For years, I had observed two opposing energies within me. How could I bridge the abyss between them? My knowledge of astrology, the ancient way, revealed intense fire—the power to burn and transform. Strong intuition, a deep longing for truth. Yet, alongside that, the shadow: a lack of self-worth, self-love, and self-respect.

On the other hand, my Moon and Mercury in Capricorn, with Luna as my ruling planet, pointed to judgment, detachment from emotions, guilt, and the wilful child who refused to grow up. Perhaps that explained why it took me so long. Capricorns tend to lock away painful emotions. They prioritize mainstream success, often at the cost of their true selves. They impose laws on others while exempting themselves, building walls around their sensitive hearts.

The combined, untamed fire of Sagittarius—amplified by Leo rising and Aries ruling my day—revealed a deep-rooted macho energy within me. And in Egypt, I had been constantly surrounded by machos. These are ancient revelations, observations I recognize in myself again and again.

I need to sit with these opposing forces—the intense search for light and the heavy weight of guilt that whispers, "You may not. There is no point in trying. Just give up." I need to consciously embrace the positive side of all this fire: the urge to shine my inner light. I need the perseverance and concentration of Capricorn and the transformative power of Luna—her wisdom, patience, and ability to let go.

And most importantly, I need to allow the wilful child within me to mature into the all-encompassing, nurturing, compassionate Mother of Life. I must learn that it is okay to give that love to myself first—so that I can share it with others from a place of abundance. I must examine my beliefs about myself, dig deep, and acknowledge them.

It's time to transform "I am not worthy. I am not good enough. I am guilty" into I AM WORTHY simply by being, by breathing, by life flowing through me. No fame, no possessions, no degrees, no titles—nothing is required to prove my worth. And guilt? Guilt is a lie. God is love, and God loves you. Even me.

All this inner processing has led me to recognize my deeply ingrained fear of the masculine—a fear intertwined with admiration and envy. I admire and envy the masculine for the power and freedom that men have enjoyed across the world since time immemorial. Yet, as a woman, I also resent them for these very privileges. My brother, simply by being born male two and a half years after me, effortlessly took over my central position as the first-born in our family. Suddenly, I was second-rate. This is where my codependent patterns, along with my guilt and feelings of unworthiness, took root. The issue of gender has always been the most profound riddle for me to resolve.

One of my spiritual teachers once told me that throughout all my incarnations, I had maintained a balance between the feminine and the masculine. But now, I realized this balance needs deep attention. I know I possess both qualities: the active, outgoing willpower and stamina for action, as well as the still, receptive, reflective, nurturing, and boundlessly creative strength of the feminine. Both aspects of myself long to be acknowledged and harmonized within me, to merge into a sacred unio mystica in the depths of my being.

Yet my admiration for the masculine has, over lifetimes, been accompanied by a deep contempt for the feminine. The scales have been off-balance for millennia. Connecting to the neutral, silent pivot point through meditation is one crucial part of my healing journey. The other is cultivating a new, fresh, and authentic understanding of gender within my mental and emotional framework.

Living near the ocean in Mexico profoundly helped me reconnect with the feminine—the cooling, soothing, cleansing, flowing energy—so different from the scorching heat of Egypt's desert, where I once gathered the light of truth to build my inner strength for transformation. Through Yemaya, I experienced healing. Earth Ma offers all her children the lessons they need for growth, consciousness shifts, and spiritual evolution. She is the greatest healer of all.

In the following weeks and lunar cycles, I committed to integrating this profound, energetic shift. I attempted to regain my stability, though I still felt wobbly, uncertain, and trembling from the shock of change.

Sacred Ayahuasca Ceremony

Then, as I faced yet another painful lesson in relationships, I found myself invited to a Sacred Ayahuasca Ceremony in Yelapa. At first, I refused—I was done with drugs. But I soon learned that Ayahuasca is not a drug; it is a sacred medicinal plant, taken in a ceremonial setting under the guidance of a shaman and his assistants. It offers a powerful opportunity for deep self-encounter and healing. Slowly, I became convinced, but I insisted on meeting the shaman first.

When he arrived with his radiant young crew, I felt an immediate sense of oneness. He was humble, kind, and deeply responsible—qualities that reassured me. Without hesitation, I said yes to Ayahuasca. I was given dietary guidelines to follow in the days leading up to the ceremony and details about the time and location. At this point, I was willing to do anything to free myself from my inner turmoil. Thank you, Universe, for this opportunity. As an offering, I paid the shaman by gifting him one of my special healing massages.

Though I still felt powerless, chaotic, and confused, when the day arrived, I prepared myself. That evening, just before dusk, I set off on a long journey. I walked along the ocean, through the village of Yelapa, and beyond—trailing up the river, past farms and another village—until finally, my heart pounding, I arrived. In the fading light, I took in the beauty of Los Naranjos, the sacred grounds where the ceremony would unfold.

People were already preparing their meditation mattresses in a circle on the floor, and there was some light food available for us in the kitchen. I was advised to get myself a bucket.

"What for?" I asked.

"You might find yourself throwing up."

Me? No way. I knew myself well—I would not throw up!

I was directed to my designated spot for meditation. Looking around, I recognized some familiar faces—good. We were told that the ceremony would continue throughout the night until dawn, and the procedure was explained to us.

Dave Roniniwe and his crew arrived and settled in, and finally, the time had come to begin. One by one, we were called to Dave's mat. He smudged our auras with sage. Then, in the next round, each of us received the magic potion—DMT—a small glass filled with it.

I lifted the glass to my nose and sniffed—hmm, a strong, herby aroma. Slowly, I raised it to my lips and took a sip, letting the liquid flow onto my tongue. I swirled it around my mouth—hmm, what a powerful taste! Earthy, green, strong—like potent medicine.

And with this benevolent introduction, our shared journey began.

I reclined on my bed under a blanket, sitting up at first. By now, Mother Night had enveloped us protectively, and I turned inward. Dave guided our journey with his shamanic music—whistling simple, melodic rhythms accompanied by gentle rattling sounds. There were noises like the wind blowing, soft voices—an entire soundscape enhancing the voyage into those ancient inner realms of healing.

Ayahuasca traveled through my body, scanning it from within. I felt her touch upon the troubled areas—pinching, squeezing swiftly, then moving on. I was completely relaxed, at ease, and surrendered.

Then, I began feeling her in my senses. Every sensory input was magnified a thousandfold. The frogs' songs became trumpeting calls, insects' buzzing pierced like needles through my brain, jungle birds sounded as if they were right inside my ears, and Dave's music resonated deeply within me.

I tried to rise and look at the night sky—wow, what a sight! Stars flashing signals, intense vibrations—a cosmic spectacle beyond words.

My skin is an open book now, absorbing a myriad of magnified vibrations. Someone starts wrenching into their bucket—oh my—then back to me, to the vibrations coursing through me. I feel myself sinking deeper and deeper within, and there she is, opening her mighty arms to envelop me in her warmest embrace. She holds me like a baby, rocking me ever so gently, whispering her love into my eager ears.

The Grand Cosmic Mother Herself cradles me, assuring me of her boundless, eternal love—just as I am, unconditionally, as her beloved child. And then, a torrent of tears bursts forth—huaaaa! I exhale years of stress, sorrow, and despair—the weight of all the effort I have carried. I release it all, moaning, groaning, and wailing, as this pent-up energy finally runs free. My sinuses clog, though water pours from my nose, and this release continues for hours. Sniffing, snorting, sobbing, surrendering—letting go of lifetimes of accumulated tension. Aaaaaaaaaaaaahhhhh—at last.

What a mighty healing is unfolding! A deep revelation: The Mother—CosMa, Aadishakti, Devi, the Source in her boundless compassion—has come to assure me that I am okay, that I am loved beyond imagination. I don't know how long this continues, but at last, exhaustion takes over. I just want to rest, perhaps sleep. Yet I still feel her within me—so gentle now—gradually ebbing away.

As night surrenders to the new day and light slowly spreads, life stirs among us once more. We pour out into the garden, where fresh fruit is served. Speechless, blissfully exhausted, we gather in quiet awe. By and by, we begin to share the sacred profundity of the experience palpable. I feel it in every being around me—this interconnectedness—this simple, blissful reality. It feels utterly true, utterly real. L O V E is the force that holds life together. That is what I feel. That is how I feel. I want to embrace everyone here and now!

Look at us—we arrived home after that long trek back from the other side of Yelapa, savoring a hearty Mexican breakfast. We looked reborn, refreshed, clear, and serene.

All day, we continued floating on this wave of bliss.

Thank you, oh Mighty Anaconda Cosmica, for revealing such sacred secrets, for gifting us your "vine of the soul", and for transforming us with your powerful magic.

I must emphasize that the Ayahuasca potion has an equally powerful ally—the music of the shamans. The rhythmic beating of drums, the rattling, the whistling and blowing, and the sweetly simple melodies of their voices all weave a spellbinding soundscape. I struggle to find words to describe them, yet I will never forget their impact on my inner world. They were the sweetest lullabies one could dream of, almost fairy-like, though no word truly captures their essence.

Let me share what one of the assistants told me when I asked how he produced such exquisite, otherworldly sounds. He explained that during his time as an apprentice, he had imbibed various plants to journey with them, and it was they who taught him their unique ways of singing and sounding. Wow! That is truly incredible.

Yes, the Ayahuasca ceremony remains an unforgettably profound experience—one that led me home to Source, to Devi, Shakti, and the essence of feminine consciousness. The challenge now is to fully embody this wisdom in my everyday life.

For those who feel drawn to this path, I encourage you to explore more—Google Ayahuasca or look into "Vine of the Soul" or "Temple of the Way of Light." This sacred plant medicine is increasingly offering itself to aid humanity in healing from disconnection, even as the Amazon rainforest is being relentlessly diminished by greed and ignorance. Nature, in her boundless compassion, continues to give.

And yet, despite this profound transformation, my mind's chaos creeps back in. My habitual thought patterns were not completely washed away with all that emotional purging. Anger resurfaces, and confusion lingers. Still, my daily tasks serve as a grounding force, and I prepare myself for another Mexican summer.

Meanwhile, my co-worker, David (pronounced "Dabeed"), has taken an interest in me. Each morning, as I step out of my room, he enjoys surprising me—grabbing me from behind and lifting me off the ground. I feel his erection pressing against my back before he playfully bites my neck. I kindly ask him to stop, making it clear that I am not interested and do not want to continue this "game." But he does not listen. Instead, he announces that once I move to the other casa, he will come to visit me. He is a genuinely sweet person, and we get along well, but he is married with children. Besides that, he could be my son. This is a clear no-go for me.

One memory stands out—something a little out of the ordinary. Every now and then, a faint, distant sound would drift through the air—a sweet, melodious tune. It would approach, then fade, then return again, moving closer and closer until, at last, a voice would call out at El Jardin's gate: "OLÁÁÁ!"

Curious, one would check to see who this mysterious visitor was, and there he would be—a deeply tanned man, his colorful garments bright against the landscape, standing with his young son. Both grinned from ear to ear, their tiny clay flutes dangling from their necks as they cheerfully asked if we had any knives in need of sharpening.

I adored those two in their simple, joyful way of celebrating life.

Blessings!

Casita and Casa Karina

El Jardín was closing for the summer, so I moved to a little casita that belonged to Karina's villa and garden. It was the sweetest little retreat you could imagine! Nestled right by the ocean, its windows remained open, inviting nature to flow freely inside. A hammock hung in front of the window overlooking the sea, and this became my favorite spot—swaying gently with a cup of coffee resting on a wooden board, watching the world unfold. Birds, iguanas, and the rhythm of nature moved in perfect harmony, creating an eternal sense of peace.

One day, as I prepared to head to Yelapa for provisions, I decided to savor a few more moments in the hammock, soaking in the breathtaking view. Finally, it was time to leave. I turned to grab my bag—and froze. To my shock, the entire interior of the casita appeared pitch black. A closer look revealed an army of ants, and in that instant, I felt them crawling up my legs. Panicked, I snatched my bag and ran, leaving behind that eerie, silent black mass without a second thought.

When I returned two hours later, I braced myself for the sight—but there was nothing. Not a single trace of blackness remained. The ants had marched through, clearing away whatever had drawn them in. I spotted them on my way back, still moving with purpose. Nature never ceases to amaze.

View of the Casita

View out of the Casita and My Favorite Hanging Spot

The gringos were leaving in May, so I went home to house-sit at Karina's villa while she spent her summers in New Mexico. I was paid to take care of the house and feed Foca, her little black sausage dog. The villa was spacious and nestled within a large tropical garden, with a small rivulet running through it. It was even farther from the village than El Jardín, the guesthouse. There were no foreigners around—only locals. The owner of the villa had once been raped in her own home.

Back at El Jardin, the first rains were imminent, hanging in the heavy, billowing clouds that had been gathering for days. As soon as the first drops fell, another phenomenon emerged, starting with a soft rustling sound from the ground. You had to watch your step now—countless land crabs scuttled out from their hiding places, swarming everywhere. It was a spectacular sight and sound! I loved playing with them; as soon as I approached, they would freeze in fear before adopting the attitude of attack as the best defence. With their tiny, round bodies and comically exaggerated grimaces, they would try to appear fierce and intimidate the intruders.

I had so much fun provoking the crabs—they looked absolutely hilarious with their tiny, expressive faces. But I never harmed them. After all, they belong to my "favorite" star sign: Cancer! My father and most of my closest relationships had been Cancers—fearful yet gentle creatures, instinctively sure in their self-defence. Somewhat elusive and secretive, they were like a smaller version of Scorpio.

Crabs are the early messengers of the rainy season, and from that moment on, I witnessed an explosion of life in nature. The mountain range across the small Bahía de Yelapa had been brown and barren for weeks. But within a week of the first rains, the trees turned yellow with blossoms, then greener and greener—a breathtaking transformation!

Back at the villa, the spectacle continued. The rains came as if the clouds had flung open some enormous gate, releasing torrents of water all at once. And with them came mighty thunderstorms! Foca, the little black sausage dog, was my living barometer—she would start trembling with fear hours before a

storm hit, and nothing could console her. Long before midnight, when the storms usually erupted in full force, she would be hiding in the farthest corner under my bed. To be honest, I often felt like joining her! The storms were ferocious as if all the wrathful forces of the universe had conspired to unleash their fury. For hours, they raged mercilessly above my little house in the Mexican wilderness. In sheer terror, I would shrink to the size of a sesame seed, mentally kneeling before God, begging for mercy, vowing never to say or do anything bad again—just please, let it stop NOW! I would tremble, shaken to my core, drenched in fear and awe.

The worst part was the lightning. Its blinding flashes pierced through closed eyelids, and the deafening crack of its impact on the tiled floor sounded like a whip lashing through the house. Oh my God, every time I heard it, I feared the next strike would hit me, reducing me to ashes. What a terrifying image of God I carried in my mind!

Meanwhile, the Mexican fishermen went out at night, unfazed by the storms. Their boats formed a circle at the boundary where the muddy river water met the ocean, knowing that's where the fish gathered. They would sit there, watching the torrential downpour and the endless sheets of lightning illuminating the sky, as if nature had put on a grand performance just for them.

It's a wonder I survived another four-month-long summer in this state of constant nighttime stress. To recover, I spent most of my days swaying in the hammock outside, watching nature explode around me. The once-gentle rivulet had become a raging torrent, reshaping the entire garden landscape. The plants, now supercharged with life, grew to enormous proportions as if trying to reclaim the world after their long, dry slumber.

River Raging as a Wild Torrent by Now!

Arachne Weaving Her Web, Oh What a Master She Is!

There was nothing else to do—the body remained drenched from dawn to dusk and beyond. I emerged from I-don't-know-where, and speaking of butterflies—wow! The garden was now teeming with them in an astonishing variety. Nature's boundless creative spirit had truly outdone itself.

My favorites were the white ones, as large as the palm of my hand, as delicate as Kleenex, and as light and graceful as angels. They were mesmerizing, a fleeting spectacle of beauty with a silent message to share: Be like me—eternally free. Leave no trace, just dance with grace, grace, grace.

What a masterpiece of creation! Each time I spotted one, I was enchanted, unable to resist dropping whatever I was doing just to follow it with my admiring gaze.

I also adored the scent of the perfect frangipani blossoms, their fragrance lingering like a whispered secret in the warm air.

Butterflies Suckling Smashed Papaya & Finishing It in No Time!

A Bird Drying Its Feathers in the Sun

Lots of Little Bright Green Baby Iguana

Down in the kitchen, we had an unexpected kind of visitor—toads!

I would often find them sitting right in the middle of Foca's food plate, big and fat, with their broad mouths dripping with small, smarty-like dry food pellets.

Foca loved them and would stare at them with a foolish expression on her face. To make matters worse, they had a terrible habit — they would leave a huge pile of mess on the kitchen floor, sit in it, and then drag herself forward, smearing the foul-smelling stuff everywhere! After that first ordeal, I made sure she became very familiar with the broom, hoping to avoid such a disgusting clean-up again.

As you can imagine, my life was full of surprises, and to top it off, there was an issue with the men. I had asked Seferino, the landowner of Karina's villa, to tell David off and forbid him from entering the premises. Sure enough, he did—but then he turned out to be interested in me! At least he went about it in a slightly more mature manner. I told him, straight up, that I had absolutely no interest—once and for all! After that, I finally had peace. He would still visit regularly, check that everything was fine in the house, drink a beer, and have a quick chat before leaving. It's much better that way!

Seferino Returning From a Successful Diving Spree to Spear Fish

Egrets & Vultures Battling for Fish Heads & Inners

I remember one particular week toward the end of summer—my time there felt almost bewitched. First, the water was gone. The tank—huge as it was—was completely empty. How? Seferino soon discovered that someone had disconnected the pipes supplying water to the tank. He fixed the issue and refilled it.

Next, there was no gas. The bottle was empty. Well, that meant Seferino had to carry a full one all the way from the village, navigating the rickety, rocky trail by foot. And those gas tanks were heavy! Sorry, Seferino! But he did it, and all was well—until the electricity went out.

No fridge. No fan. No computer. No lights. Nothing. Believe it or not, we endured this for more than a week—it was borderline torture. The cause? An explosion in the main electricity tower had taken out the entire power system in Yelapa. Fixing it was no small feat, especially under extreme weather conditions deep in the jungle above the villa. Finally, the power was restored—but at a cost. The initial surge of electricity was so strong that hundreds of devices were fried on the spot. A common occurrence in rural Mexico, apparently. Piles of useless fridges, freezers, computers, fans, and AC units were loaded onto boats—the same ones that had brought them in—only to be dumped onto an ever-growing heap of electronic waste. Amen.

My computer? Gone. Completely dead. No sign of life. All my files—vanished, except for the ones I had saved on flash drives.

Then, as if all that wasn't enough, came the announcement of an approaching hurricane. Because, why not? Feverish preparations began. Everyone scrambled to minimize the damage—but from what, exactly? I had never experienced a hurricane before. From the storm? The flood? The unleashed fury of the elements? And how exactly do you keep the elements out when the house is designed to be open on all sides?

I did my best and followed Karina's instructions. Since the villa sat low and close to the ocean, I was invited to stay with a couple who lived higher up. I gladly accepted. We sat glued to the weather updates, waiting. At one point, someone arrived from the village and reported that two people were sitting on the beach, drinking beer, and waiting for the hurricane to hit. Crazy folk!

Then came the news—the hurricane had changed direction. We lingered, waiting for confirmation. The air felt different. The tension eased. I returned home to tend to the animals. Two days later, I finally got the call: the danger had passed. Yelapa had been spared this time.

Relief. Relaxation. Back to normal. But had we missed out on something? Maybe.

Throughout it all, I kept up with my meditation and yoga. I ate well—fresh, healthy food. I read through some of the books in Karina's library, mostly on Buddhist principles. They were enlightening. I also found material on codependency and worked my way through it.

Casa Papellion and Casa Milagros

Karina threw me out of her house as soon as I returned—over a minor disagreement. The Mexicans called her the Ice Princess. She was wealthy but trapped in a cycle of addiction and depression, which made her both ignorant and arrogant. No one could get close to her; warmth simply was not in her nature. I felt like I had to handle her like a raw egg, and when I didn't, she reacted. I always sensed she was jealous of me, though I never understood why.

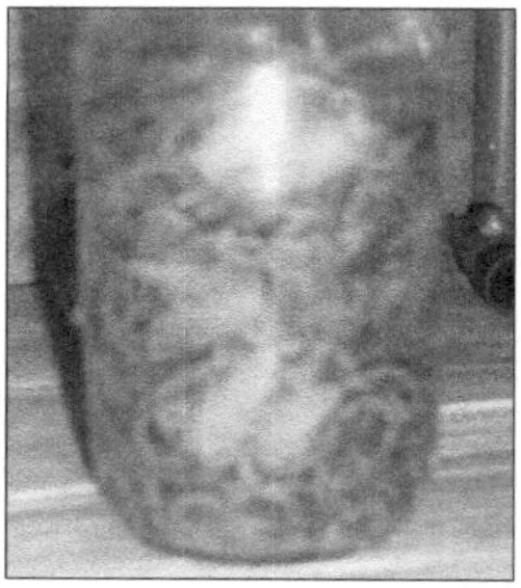

So, I gathered my things—actually relieved to be free of her energy—and made my way up the steep hill across from her garden gate to Casa Papellion. Thomas, kind enough to offer me temporary shelter in his beautiful open house, welcomed me. From high above, the house overlooked the ocean, a breathtaking view. He told me I could stay until his girlfriend arrived. On his kitchen counter, he kept a glass filled with scorpions he had found around the house. Of course, scorpions thrive in rocky areas with plenty of moisture!

Now, I needed to find a place among people who were more welcoming. That's when I met Jaime, a wild young Mexican electrician with a knack for mischief. He had a habit of sneaking up behind people and making an eerily realistic donkey sound—so convincing that when you turned around, it was shocking to see him instead of an actual donkey!

Jaime, as He Likes to See Himself!

His mother owned Casa Milagros, the House of Wonders, a guesthouse perched on the edge of a rocky hill jutting into the ocean, offering a spectacular view of Yelapa Bay.

Casa Milagros

It was a breathtaking spot, accessible by a trail that wound up from the village, counting 182 solid rock steps through the dense jungle. I don't remember exactly how I ended up there, but I did. The first time I climbed that trail, I was panting and out of breath, but the feeling was incredible—my lungs felt wide open, my body vibrant with energy! I loved it.

Antonia offered me a place to stay in exchange for work—food and accommodation in a small, humble room. I gladly agreed. For the rest of my time in Mexico, I lived at Casa

Milagros, chasing scorpions with a broom, cleaning and resetting rooms, and doing the laundry. I was also able to offer massages, allowing me to earn a little money on the side.

Finally, my life began to stabilize, and as money slowly started to flow in, things felt normal again.

View from Casa Milagros Top Deck towards the Baja

In my free time, I would sit on the upper deck, gazing out over Yelapa Bay, watching the vast body of water breathe. For many blissful hours, I sat there, witnessing the quiet rhythms of nature. It became my favorite pastime.

During this time, I discovered A Course in Miracles and slowly worked my way through it. It's an incredible book! I had owned a copy back in 1984 but sold it without ever reading it. Looking back, I wish I had.

What I see while Enjoying My Morning Coffee

We had wonderful guests, many of whom were professional bird watchers, fully equipped with binoculars, cameras, and a wealth of knowledge—especially about the local birds. Thanks to them, I saw many species I had never noticed before; they could spot birds instantly, no matter how dense the foliage.

They pointed out a few small species and the majestic falcons that lived nearby—we saw them almost daily. I especially loved watching the pelicans; what magnificent birds they are! So many more feathered visitors came to our lofty perch above the village. Pelicans, in particular, fascinated me—not only for their grace in flight but also for their deep symbolism. They are known for their self-sacrifice for their young, and their synchronized flight is a breathtaking sight.

From our vantage point, the view stretched across the Baja, with the mountain range to the north and Puerto Vallarta visible to the right.

The village! Of course, I visited often, as it was where I got my provisions. Over time, I became acquainted with some of the locals and a few of the American expatriates living there. However, I preferred the Mexicans for their straightforward, down-to-earth nature, their dry yet friendly demeanor, their sharp sense of humor, and their street smartness. They live simple family lives under the protection of the Madonna, the Virgin Mary, who is their primary source of strength and the focus of their worship and prayers.

During one particularly inquisitive visit to a church service in their modest Catholic church, I was surprised to see that women played a leading role in all the activities. The service was lively and filled with humor, though tinged with a certain bias that, it seemed, was an inseparable part of the broader Christian experience.

After their day's work, the boys would trot off to the "hospital"—which, in their case, meant gathering at the local supermarket to drink beer. Whatever gave them a high, they used to break the monotony of their otherwise routine lives. In this, their situation was comparable to that of the fellahin in Upper Egypt.

One more thing I almost forgot to mention, which greatly impressed me, is the sheer size of the trees in the Mexican jungle! They are enormous, casting generous shade, bearing delicious fruit in perfect timing, providing homes for birds, and radiating a majestic, graceful life force to all who have the eyes to see. They are truly amazing beings! There is so much more to say about nature and my deep admiration for her.

Of course, I also meet wonderful people. Yet, my interest in human interactions is far less pronounced; I much prefer solitude in the healing embrace of nature. Once again, I was reminded of how many people—including myself—are in need of healing.

Too many mirrors reflect pain, addiction, depression, and despair. I felt that such reflections did me little good.

As a species, we have gone astray—far astray. I am seeking the road home, the path to restoring order within.

In 1987 and 1989, I staged a performance titled The Goddesses Return to Dance Again, taking on the roles of organizer, author, and dancer/actress. But where is that goddess within me now—slumbering, waiting to awaken?

I studied Ancient Egypt, Vedic Tantra, and Taoist roots, along with women's immortality practices. In The Play of Consciousness, Swami Muktananda wrote about HER—Shakti, the consort of Shiva, the Divine Mother. I quote:

Chitshakti is completely free. She performs all actions and gives the fruit of all spiritual disciplines. She bestows both worldly fulfillment and liberation.

Self-luminous, transcending time, space and form, she is the creative aspect of Parashiva, the basis of all forms and energy.

It is she who gives grace, and she who controls it. She is the illuminator of transcendental reality. She is both worldly and spiritual life. She is the knowledge of the enlightened and the fruit of action of the active. She is the ecstatic state of Bhaktas and the dynamic Kundalini of yogis.

She is the beauty of the whole world!!!

Everything that happens in the world is CHITI.

Enter into the repose of Chiti. The supreme Shakti lives within you in her 5 aspects: consciousness, bliss, volition, knowledge and action.

Renounce the very notion of differentiation—the "I." Then, Chiti can be seen flowing through all the sense organs and their objects. No more "me," "I," or "mine"! Never perceive anything as separate from Spirit/Shakti. The vision of undifferentiated ONENESS dissolves all multiplicity and duality.

The enlightened one sees the world as a play of Chiti, accepting the consequences of their actions with the understanding that the world is the very light of their Self.

I observe that I still differentiate by defining gender separately, yet I know that in Higher Consciousness, this distinction dissolves into thin air. And still, I find it essential to integrate both masculine and feminine attributes into ONE PURE CONSCIOUSNESS—no more division. Shiva and Shakti are aspects of the same DIVINE INTELLIGENT CREATIVE ENERGY.

Leaving Europe for Nigeria in 1987 felt like returning to an ancient comfort zone of my soul. Leaving again for Egypt in 2005 was a similar experience. Both journeys challenged my physical comfort. Crossing the Atlantic to the West meant leaving behind the old worlds—and with them, all my comfort zones—body, mind, soul, and spirit.

I sensed it, and I was ready—no matter the cost. I was prepared to have all my safeguards shattered, to be stripped bare until only pure, raw beingness remained. I faced my fears—big and small—and allowed them to dissolve.

More and more, I surrendered. I let go and fell into my natural power, energy, and wisdom—resisting nothing, wanting nothing, seeking only truth. I came to understand that my natural "I AM" is always my true Self. It was my mental-emotional body and psychological conditioning that created the illusion of separation. Concepts, laws, regulations, and attachments distort perception. The constructed "me," which once served to ensure my survival as an infant, is far from who I truly AM. The expectation that life exists to provide happiness and fulfillment—ha!—so long as trauma lingers buried in the subconscious, I experience constriction.

Over the past ten years, I renounced everything—love relationships, belongings, even my most cherished collection of musical instruments and my vast, revered pile of books. All those countless Faustian collections of wisdom, "black on white," that still left me a fool for far too long! I left my home, job, and friends—again and again. Then, I found myself sweeping floors, cleaning rooms, and making beds in exchange for shelter and food.

And that—THAT—is where the light enters. Diamonds are formed in darkness, under immense pressure!

Depression and despair—the dark voids that once regularly pulled me into their hopeless gloom—are now but distant memories, as are the intense sparks of hopeful enthusiasm that used to ignite a million times over, driving me to move mountains—more for others than for myself! I would summon every ounce of energy within me, only to crash against life's indifference, tumbling right back into those foggy, swamp-like depths of despair. A relentless seesaw! My life has always oscillated between these extreme poles. It's a wonder that I wasn't torn apart.

What saved me was an undeniable awareness of a higher state of being. My spiritual studies and practices—however diverse and varied—nurtured an inner foundation, steadily building a sense of stability. But my struggle lay in my deep identification with my restless, ever-creative, and extremely opinionated monkey mind! A will of iron drove me—I wanted to be the first to achieve enlightenment—haaaaaahahahahahaha!

God, how I stressed over it! Devil, what supreme folly! Thank goodness for the humor in life!

It seems I had to think my way through all the wisdom I encountered, arriving at understanding only through direct experience. And yet, I excelled at confusing myself—absorbing insights from countless sources, applying them literally and vigorously, and expecting instant results while simultaneously feeding my doubts. Pulled in every direction, torn apart by contradictions. Even writing this now makes me feel dizzy. What did I do to myself? My ego—desperate to maintain control—blinded me for years. I was a master of self-deception, circling endlessly in the labyrinth of my own mind. How destructive, how ignorant these mental traps are! Oh Lord, have mercy on me!

And then—Mexico. Yes, Mexico! Your paradise revealed my inner hell. A total disintegration of the self I thought I was. I became a mess—a holy mess. How do I find my way out? I am so confused! And yet, to the outside world, I held it together. With clenched teeth, I stumbled through my internal chaos, keeping up a façade of control. A defence mechanism—stay back, don't come too close, don't wound me further. And still, life carried on.

I must share my magical encounter with a Praying Mantis at Casa Milagros:

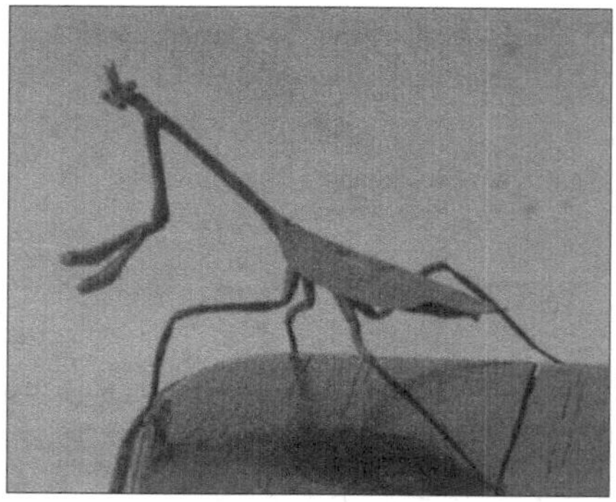

A Praying Mantis

There she was, perched at the edge of the dining table, staring at me intently, tracking my every move, a delicate crown adorning her tiny head. An incredible little creature—an auspicious messenger!

On One of My Last Days up at Casa Milagros, This Double Rainbow Graced Us with Its Radiance – Wow!

I love the silent solitude of nature, with all its unique sounds, abundant company, and radiant beauty. Am I a hermit? Here, my mind has to confront only its own boundaries and limitations—and for now, that's enough. It feels like a city of 25 million people—so many walls, roads, and regulations. And yet, I do love people. Natural, simple, community-oriented people, as I meet them on my journeys. I easily adapt to their ways, and my neurotic Western city-dweller habits seem to disappear without a trace. I am like a chameleon; I don't carry a cultural identity that immediately marks me as German wherever I go. I had efficiently locked away my "German-ness" during my years in Italy, Nigeria, and Egypt. But in Azania and Mexico, it has started to break through again. Interesting. My deep affinity for Africa and its people is no secret—neither to myself nor to those who know me.

The other day, a familiar question resurfaced in my mind: How do I heal my long-standing wounds of betrayal and abandonment? These themes have echoed through all my relationships. Sometimes, I was the one who inflicted them. What a mighty quest. I considered seeking professional help. Then it dawned on me—hey, honey, you've been dealing with all your struggles on your own; you CAN handle this one, too! The answer, as it turns out, was surprisingly simple: STOP BETRAYING AND ABANDONING YOURSELF!

Of course, breaking that chronic pattern is still a challenge—but I am trying. I have successfully resisted thousands of handsome young stallions wooing me in Egypt. I have let go of two unsuitable New World descendants here in Mexico with ease. And don't even mention the Mexicans—there is no space for such games in my life. No. I am firmly on the path of self-respect in every aspect of life. Vigilance, being present in every moment, is my tool. Smiling to my liver. Thinking with my heart. Moving toward my destiny. End of betraying myself.

Let's See Where Life Takes Me Next

I was in Mexico without a return ticket. Earning enough money to buy one would take longer than I wanted to stay. So, I asked my elderly father to send me a ticket back to Germany. He didn't.

Then, someone offered me a job managing her guesthouse in Guanajuato, a lively inland town just a few hours' drive from paradise. It didn't interest me in the slightest. After some time, I asked my father again. This time, he said: COME HOME!

I found a cheap ticket and finally prepared to leave my paradise. Another summer under this inferno? No, thanks. Truthfully, I've never been drawn to beach life. My heart has always been pulled toward a more spiritual existence. A few people joined my meditation sessions in Yelapa, but it wasn't something I could build a life on.

Returning home to my father was a thought I had been nurturing, painting in my mind with beautiful images—the house, the garden, the chance to be with him and care for him. Yes, I was ready. Egypt still lingers in my soul despite the paradise of Mexico. Yet, I am making plans to return to Yelapa one day—this time with many guests.

Taking off from Yelapa Boat Station, Bye Bye Casa Milagros!

I packed my things, and on the morning of February 14, 2012, I left Yelapa with far less than I had arrived. I crossed the Baja by boat, saying one last goodbye to the paradise that had been my home for two rich years. In Puerto Vallarta, I took a taxi to the airport. Soon, the plane lifted me into the sky, offering one final view of that stunningly beautiful tropical landscape. I waved goodbye in my heart—even to the vultures near the airport, which I had once mistaken for eagles.

LOVE

Is a four-letter word,
Much abused as a sword—in ignorance.
LOVE
Searched after by all—often ending in FALL,
Misreading the call to search for its M Y S T E R Y.
We enjoy love's sweet ointment and suffer its disappointment,
But remain ever hungry for more of this war...
S T O P! E V O L - V E!
RESOLVE the race!
Embrace in grace and face, amazed, A L L of life!
T O G E T H E R
Enter the flow—allow it to grow.
Be a galaxy—enjoy the dance—entranced.
Feel how you are free—in deep unity.
Love unbound—so profound.
Re-sound!
Dive deep and climb steep—be soaked and cloaked.
In the T A O—Yin-Yang.
One song—bliss and harmony!
IsIs 2009

Thank you, Mexico, for an unforgettable time in your breathtaking, healing paradise—and for the healing crisis I finally surrendered to. Thank you, ever-generous Mother Nature. And finally, thank you, mighty Anaconda Cosmica, for your healing kisses! I bow to you all in deepest reverence.
Farewell, beautiful Bahía de Banderas.

MexCity

Daddy-sitting in Hamburg

My journey took me to Frankfurt via Mexico City and Cancún. As we approached Mexico City, I gasped at the sheer vastness of this sprawling metropolis, nestled within a ring of mountains yet extending far beyond them—an awe-inspiring sight. Then came Cancún, with its lush jungle landscape, coconut palms lining white sandy beaches, and sun-drenched holiday resorts. But the sunshine was nowhere to be found when I landed in Düsseldorf. From there, a final short flight took me to Hamburg, where, unsurprisingly, it was raining.

I couldn't wait to see my Dad. My brother had given me a subtle warning, and now I understood why. My father, now 90, had aged in more ways than one. He seemed frail but was genuinely overjoyed to see me—and the feeling was mutual. Moving about with difficulty, burdened by his corpulent frame, he struggled to remember where he had parked his car in the large airport lot. We wandered around until, at last, we spotted it. Once inside, we set off for home—a mere 10-minute drive away.

And so, welcome back—to the very place where all your patterns first took shape.

Daddy on July 2012; He Was 91 Then

My brother passed by, cloaked in his usual shield of arrogance, and delivered the most important information with a cynical undertone. He, too, did not radiate contentment—or anything close to it. Now a government director working in Hamburg's Senate for Finances, he earned a good income. Yet his long-time companion had developed dementia at the age of 64, becoming an immense burden on him in every possible way. He felt responsible for her but struggled to comprehend her fate, suffering deeply as a result.

Beyond that, he had once developed a small malignant growth on his knee. The doctors mishandled the situation—removing it, subjecting him to a year of chemotherapy—and I watched as he lost all physical and psychological strength. He remained insistent in following modern medicine, completely indifferent to my advice to seek out a more natural resolve. Ultimately, after repeated issues with his leg and a failed operation, he made a shocking decision: he had it amputated. But that was not the end of his troubles—far from it. To this day, he continues to suffer.

If you allow yourself to be ruled by fear, your decisions will only lead to greater despair. But my brother was not just ruled by fear. There was something deeper. Our mother's brother had lost his leg due to a war injury, and my mother always spoke of him with admiration, even reverence. He had an impressive presence—strong, capable, and "just fine" despite his loss. I suspect that, on a subconscious level, my brother longed for that same admiration from our mother, leading him to make a drastic decision without hesitation. And still today, his choice of companions is deeply neurotic. He remains trapped in the patterns our mother instilled in him—inclined toward self-destruction, with a tendency toward alcoholism. What a family I grew up in!

So, I took matters into my own hands. The house was no longer as it had been under my mother's watchful eye. She had passed away in December 2008, completely demented by the end, unable to recognize me on my last visit. My father and brother had cared for her. My father bore the brunt of the responsibility, tending to her day and night. She had been restless, constantly moving up and down the stairs, until one day, she fell and broke her hip. She was taken to the hospital, never waking from anesthesia. She had been scheduled to move into a nursing home the very next day, but she had clung to my father with all she had. He had been her provider, and she supported his career as best as possible. Though she had often cried for a divorce, she never took any steps toward it—she was entirely dependent on him.

For years, they had employed a "house pearl" to keep things in order. When I arrived, she was on high alert—and with good reason. It didn't take long for me to sense something was off, and I started questioning her. Reflecting now, I realize there were many things I initially overlooked. While she had indeed provided my father with companionship in his sudden loneliness after my mother's death, she had also taken advantage of his vulnerable state. She neglected her duties, overcharged him, and ultimately exploited the situation.

So there I was, needing to realign things with my father's best interests. Many battles followed, with my brother involved as well. In the end, she had to go. Her services were no longer needed, and her demands were simply unacceptable.

I decided to get a job at the airport, found one within ten days, and replaced the "Pearl's" services with my own care for the entire household—shopping, cooking, cleaning, and more. Thank God my brother had arranged home care for Dad long ago. The caregivers helped him out of bed in the mornings, washed and dressed him, and prepared his breakfast. This was a great relief, and despite some initial misunderstandings, we eventually developed a good working relationship.

My father was apprehensive about me. He clearly disliked how I took charge of things, and he was annoyed that I had let the "Pearl" go. I cared for him as best as I could while living in my mother's tiny old sewing room under the roof. Meanwhile, his office occupied the best room in the house, complete with a sunlit terrace overlooking our beautiful garden. Day after day, he would say, "I must work in my office and finish this book." But he never once went in.

The house was in complete disarray, a chaotic mess. Dad had truly lost his grasp on things—he was forgetful about almost everything except for his cherished memories of his childhood home in Amberg. I tried many ways to engage him, entertain him, even amuse or interest him, but most efforts were in vain. Eventually, I realized he was resisting my directness. I had always been the one to notice when things were going wrong, and I had always been resented for it. My father was a master of denial. A true patriarch, he subtly dominated every woman around him, charming them all with his gentleness and kindness—everyone except me. I saw through it. And though I did not always resist openly, I did so in my own way.

Then, everything escalated with the arrival of my sister, six years younger than me, who had been living in Portugal for 20 years. I went to pick her up at the airport, and what I saw left me in shock. She was a wreck—shaking from head to toe, emaciated, and missing several teeth. She was weak, barely able to carry her small suitcase. I knew she had been an alcoholic since she was 14—42 years now—but seeing her in this state was gut-wrenching. A mix of compassion and frustration churned within me. I took her home and witnessed my father's exuberant welcome, their intimate closeness cutting me deeply. He still pampered her endlessly while I remained Cinderella—expected to toil for them all.

Rage boiled inside me, and I had plenty of reasons for it during her visit. Yet, I played along and held my tongue—for a while. I cared for her as best as I could, but she repeatedly crossed my boundaries. Eventually, I spoke my mind, confronting her about her lifestyle. It was pointless. She openly admitted she would never stop drinking. And then, to my disbelief, she convinced our father to drive to a wine dealer and buy her an entire carton of expensive wine. On his way back, while carrying the box down to the basement, he tripped on the stairs. I found him lying flat on his face, bleeding from his head. At that moment, I wanted to shake some sense into him.

And so the cycle continued—over and over—until I finally realized I had to protect myself. My sister had a way of sneaking into my psyche, manipulating me with her bottomless neediness, her lies, and betrayals. This had to stop. She left for Portugal more than once, unable to cope with my energy, only to return and restart the same game. But I quit playing. I focused on my own needs. Many times, I was ready to leave that house for good. But I stayed, recognizing I wasn't quite ready yet.

One battle I did win: reclaiming my father's untouched office as my own living space. With some furniture rearranging and book-packing, I emptied the office, repainted it, laid new carpeting, and bought my own furniture from Ikea. At last, I had what I deserved—a beautiful, peaceful sanctuary where I could shut the door behind me. My brother supported me and helped finance the transformation. It was a victory.

Meanwhile, my first job ended when the company went bankrupt, but I quickly retrained as an airport masseuse specializing in acupressure for travellers. I loved the work, and it paid well—another victory. My brother acknowledged my sense of responsibility but criticized my inability to handle the "shit" that inevitably came my way in that household. But this victory had strengthened me.

Gradually, my relationship with Dad shifted. I poured genuine love and care into making him happy. I listened to his old stories—stories I had heard a thousand times. I shared my feelings about everything happening around us. His understanding was limited, as was his hearing. When I raised my voice, he would snap, "Don't shout like that!" He was subtly aggressive—always so subtle and completely unaware of it.

But I was done swallowing my frustrations. I expressed myself plainly, whether he understood or not. At that point, it was about preserving my own sanity in this madhouse.

His condition declined subtly. Many times, he fell down the staircase. It was a wonder he never hurt himself more seriously—just a wound on his head, which was bad enough. We had to move him to the dining room on the ground floor, but he still refused to use the toilet chair. Instead, he would sneak down the stairs to the basement and the second bathroom to relieve himself—and often, he didn't make it in time. I understood his motivation, but his safety was our biggest concern.

God, what a stubborn man he was! But beyond all of this, I realized how deeply I loved him, and I felt blessed to spend his final years caring for him. We laughed together often. Though he didn't always trust my sense of humor—perhaps thinking I was laughing at him—it wasn't true. Well, maybe sometimes, when he came out with the most unexpected, out-of-the-blue remarks. I couldn't help but burst into spontaneous laughter.

I cared for him until I was utterly exhausted—after countless hospital visits due to his falls, both down and even up the stairs. Eventually, my brother and I decided that he would be safer and better cared for in a nursing home. He resisted, though he understood. He recalled the struggles of caring for my mother and dreaded the thought. My brother arranged for a free room in the same home where his companion was now staying. We sold our family home of 50 years to our good neighbors, and for the first time in ages, I was free to live my life again.

Immediately, I flew to Cairo. During that time, my dad nearly died while trying to acclimate to his new environment. I needed a break. But he survived and, over time, found his new surroundings increasingly interesting.

Clearing out the family house was emotionally and physically draining. My attempt to save some of its treasures was cut short by the pressing need to clear everything out completely. In the end, it all landed in the trash—a grand lesson in letting go.

I was happy to have my life back and with a nice sum of money in my bank account, yet on another level, something about what we had done didn't feel entirely right. We had broken the continuity. But then again, that had happened before—not by my hand, but by the passage of time, by the ignorance of their generation.

Dad was terrified of dying. Many times, he would clutch my hand, his nails digging into my flesh, clinging to life. He was scared. I tried to console him, reminding him of the rich and wonderful life he had lived—something to be grateful for. I told him that no one survives forever, that we merely cross over for a little rest before continuing our journey in another way. He would look at me with disdain and say, "He who believes is blessed." And I would reply, "Exactly. That's how it is. And he who does not believe cannot be blessed." In the end, he was left to his fate by his own choice, and I had done my best.

As it turned out, I was spared from holding his hand in his final moments. That pained me for a while, but eventually, I let go. I finally freed myself from the lifelong feeling of responsibility I had carried for him. It was time to move on.

May his gentle and lovable soul be blessed all the same. We meet, and we part—that's life. Goodbye, Dad, until we meet again.

He is still with me and within me. True love never dies.

He passed away at the age of 94 on March 20, 2016. I will never know the exact circumstances of his departure, but does it really matter? What matters is that I have much to be grateful for—what I received from and through him. He was a wonderful, loyal, and caring father, and in today's world, that is an invaluable gift.

Thank you, beloved Dad, for all you were and all you did for me. I forgive your human flaws, and I love you for eternity. I hope to meet you there.

Dad on His 94th Birthday with My Friend Angel,
Who Streamed Him Regularly with JSJ

My sister lost her long-term life partner, who slowly withered away due to the long-term effects of alcohol abuse. She still lives in Portugal, but I have no connection with her. I found some solace in knowing that a whole truckload of belongings from my father's house had made its way to Portugal.

My brother got married at the age of 64 in a grand, pompous ceremony. I did not attend. His lifestyle and values had always been the complete opposite of mine, and I no longer wished to pretend otherwise. I was done playing games—once and for all. Wishing him a happy married life!

It reminded me of something I once read about Western white civilization: that it is an infantile life design. I wholeheartedly agree. White nations have created an artificial, delusional existence, completely detached from existential reality. Uprooted, unearthed, misguided, deluded—Shivji, is this Your doing?

It was 2014, and at the age of 64, I was back in Egypt, starting over once again—leaving Europe for good!

The Dual Nature of Mind

The human mind,
Unique in its kind—its dual nature,
Serving fear or serving love.
Human life, a constant struggle,
An ever-rocking boat:
Will you drown, or will you float?
Or even rise above?
Humankind has the power—
And this is the calling of THIS hour—
To rise out of masking disguise, all the way now,
To its true spirit essence.
The path is open—make your decision
Of WHO is the master in your human house!
Create a balance of hemispheres,
Of distinction and intuition.
Connect to the heart
And unite what drifted apart.
Duality is but illusion,
Causing all our worldly confusion.
ONENESS IS eternally present.
It IS what IS—the source of life!
Now, strive and relax!
What a paradox!

IsIs 2010

Meeting India in Egypt

A healer in Germany—upon learning that I was about to move back to Egypt—gave me the phone number of a Facebook friend of hers living in Cairo, saying she felt he would be a key connection for me there.

Once I arrived in Cairo, I called him. We met, and he invited me to a meditation session in Al-Azhar Park—a beautiful, elevated spot that feels like an island amidst a vast ocean of buildings. It is an oasis of greenery, featuring various bodies of water and restaurants, while the minarets of mosques and rocky remnants of the desert rise in the distance, creating a breathtaking view.

On a gently sloping patch of grass, we found a small group preparing a blanket for us all to sit on. Among them was Madhu, the meditation guide—a young Indian woman with long, jet-black hair, a colorful dress, and a warm, radiant smile. She embraced me spontaneously, her soft, fleshy body exuding warmth, and we clicked instantly!

Just Arrived!

This was the beginning of a long journey together. Later, Madhu invited me to stay with her and her husband, Ram, in their vast, spacious apartment in the lush green suburbs of Maadi.

Meditation became our daily "bread." The Indian home-cooked vegetarian meals nourished my soul, while circles of Indian neighbors, along with Egyptian and foreign visitors, came together to share the joy of diving within. Twice a year, MadhuRam's Indian master visited with a group of disciples to experience a two-hour private meditation in the so-called Cheops Pyramid's King's Chamber. He shared profound teachings—mainly on the purpose and benefits of meditation, the virtues of vegetarianism and holistic health, and the power of pyramids.

I found many more books to devour, satisfying my hunger for knowledge. Yet, the most precious part of my time with MadhuRam and the wide circle of friends was the open space of acceptance—non-judgmental, joyous togetherness filled with laughter. Life was easy, yet now deeply rooted in spiritual practice.

My Wonderful Hosts Madhu and Ram

Here, I found myself in a field of healing—a space where I could finally relax and recover after two challenging years of caring for my dad. I had nothing to do but simply be with myself, embraced by an open, free, and non-attached way of connecting—where we related as sisters and brothers in spirit, free from conflict or entanglement. Wow—what a gift! In this sacred space, my soul could heal even more. Thank you, Spirit!

My First Trip to India

Madhu took me on my first trip to India, visiting the southern cities of Hyderabad and Bangalore. The traffic was overwhelmingly noisy and chaotic, with vehicles rushing aggressively and people crowding the streets like ants on a hill. Yet, the streets were vibrant, bursting with a myriad of colors and designs, especially in the traditional attire of Indian women. It was breath-taking—a true feast for the eyes and soul, nourished by beauty and color.

The days spent in the ashram were imbued with peace. I encountered many warm-hearted and open Indian people, enjoyed fresh coconuts—heavenly gifts—several times a day, and savored tropical fruits. Walking through the campus, I paused at various meditation sites, admiring the abundant nature in all its forms—sights, sounds, scents, and, once again, colors. We also traveled to Kerala, where we spent three wonderful days in the jungle on a coffee farm.

At the Patriji Pyramid Valley Campus, I observed that most people were engaged in intellectual and spiritual activities, which did not particularly draw me in. However, I fondly recall one outing beyond the ashram gates with Madhu. From a distance, we spotted an enormous banyan tree. Its massive trunk seemed large enough to live in, while its branches extended in all directions, with aerial roots growing downward, forming a vast, natural umbrella. Beneath it, one could sit and absorb the profound energy of this ancient being—one that had been worshipped for centuries and had witnessed countless lives come and go.

We also visited the sacred cows, leisurely munching grass, privileged in their revered status within this blessed land of Bharat. Along the way, we met simple farmers dressed in white dhotis, their black eyes glowing with warmth and respect.

Overall, my first experience of Bharat left a deep impression. It reassured me that its ancient traditions remain very much alive in rural communities. However, I also learned one crucial lesson—I would never again visit India in May! The sweltering 46°C heat combined with over 80% humidity completely overwhelmed my body. BOOM. I survived, though!

Interestingly, this first encounter with India reminded me a lot of Africa—the red soil, the lush greenery, and the dramatic landscape scattered with massive rocks. Majestic acacia trees stood proudly, their flamboyant blossoms blazing like fiery torches under the sun. Falcons soared high above in slow, graceful circles, their cries marking dawn and dusk as they gathered atop tall trees—or even city rooftops—to exchange messages. I saw them everywhere, even in the bustling cities, carving out their own space in the sky. I love falcons—their royal bearing, their effortless glide, their tranquil yet powerful presence. They are the true kings of the skies! Watching them drill into the heavens, gliding effortlessly on the wind's currents, made me long for that same freedom. Ah, to be like an eagle—just spread my wings and sail upon the breath of heaven!

But back to reality, deep within me, I still carry an unresolved knot. Meditation in the grand pyramids of Pyramid Valley, Bangalore, and Kadthal, Hyderabad, did not reach those inner depths. It remained just another worldly experience.

And yet, this was my first taste of ancient Bharat—long overdue and unforgettable.

Aadhivaralakshmi and Her Sweet Husband

In Kadthal, at Patriji's center near Hyderabad, I rented a room with an Indian couple in their hand-made home on the fringe of the ashram grounds. Their house, built entirely from natural materials in an ancient, traditional style, was surrounded by a breath-taking garden filled with vibrant scents, colors, and an abundance of delicious fruits, herbs, and fluttering butterflies. What a heavenly, tranquil spot! And what loving souls they were! I deeply cherished their mostly silent company—our conversations were limited by language, as their English was minimal, and I had no knowledge of any Indian language—but their warmth and hospitality spoke louder than words. Their only neighbors were peacocks, whose haunting cries echoed through the mornings.

One day, on a leisurely walk to the Grand Kadthal Pyramid, we encountered a peacock not far from our path. It darted away in a half-flight, half-running manner, its long tail feathers brushing against the bushes. It was a vision of pure majesty as if proclaiming - I love and honor who I am!

Leaving behind this peaceful, simple life and my gracious hosts was not easy. I could have stayed forever, but it is best to say farewell while joy still lingers. Our flight was bound for Cairo, and so I waved goodbye to them, but I knew I would carry them in my heart always.

Back in Cairo, I found myself appreciating the slow, laid-back rhythm of life, even in the bustling city. By contrast, India felt like a boiling cauldron of energy—alive, vibrant, and always in motion. The traffic in its cities was chaotic, fast-paced, and almost aggressive, with honking filling the air as drivers weaved their way through the dense streets. The rhythms of India pulsed with life—its colorful temples stood open and filled with worshippers, and its markets overflowed with an endless display of wares that ignited my curiosity time and time again. There was no limit to exploration in India—abundance surrounded me in every possible way! And the food—oh my!

Of course, modernity has made its way into Indian cities, but it feels like a thin veneer over a civilization rooted in traditions that stretch back tens of thousands of years. Had I come here in my 20s or 30s, I might have been completely absorbed into this vast, exhilarating culture, so vastly different from Europe's safe, sterile, and predictable way of life. India is a challenge—but also an endless blessing.

During my journey, I read A Fine Balance, the longest book I had ever dared to take on. It had me in tears one moment and rolling with laughter the next. At times, I was frozen in terror at the sheer depth of human suffering described within its pages. Yet, through its stories, I found another kind of introduction to India's profoundly transformative culture—one deeply anchored in Sanatana Dharma, the eternal, natural laws of life.

Human Mind - The Devil

The devil wears two horns on his head,
And he is red, as is Seth!
Well, the battle between the polar forces
Brings about the generation of life
As a way for humans to learn to thrive
In the Higher Taste way—
Most delicate balance!
The devil is known as the whisperer,
A master at tempting the virtuous into vices.
In this way, he's known to add some spices to life.
Many love to go to hell because of the delicious parties—
Sex, drugs, and rock 'n' roll!
Whereas in heaven, they only pray all day!
A naively distorted image, this is, of course.
In truth, much more is at stake!
Evolution of consciousness is on,
Being creative in more evolved ways—supportive of life!
Seth still might stick his redhead in
To help us BEWARE of him within!
He loves the Creator perhaps more than we do—
Only shows his love in his own tricky ways!
Esu, the trickster—they appease him FIRST!
Esu, we love you; you bring about thirst—for Light!
When the partying is done… and all the funny fun…
IsIs 2010

TIRUVANNAMALAI – Arunachala

Upon realizing that Patriji's path could not fully satisfy my inner quest, I turned once again to Sri Ramana Maharshi. I read every book I could find about Him and by Him, deeply connecting with His teachings. His words resonated within me, shaping my inner space, and I felt inspired to spend time at His ashram in Tiruvannamalai, Tamil Nadu, India, in December 2014.

Sri Ramana Maharshi continuously inspires seekers to ask: WHO AM I?

I understood that I was not the body, the mind, the five senses, or the emotions. I was the Self—pure and perfect. But how could I find the Self? How could I touch upon it? Sitting in silent meditation did not provide the answer. A restless voice still echoed within me, cutting through the silence. Yes, I had experienced moments of stillness many times before, but there was always a lingering "but"—an undercurrent of unnecessary thoughts rolling through my mind.

My experience of Tiruvannamalai and the sacred mountain of Arunachala, an embodiment of Shiva, Mahadeva, was one of pure joy—at times, even bliss. The little town pulsed with a strong, positive energy—a love-filled vibration. Smiling faces greeted me everywhere, both among the locals and the many seekers from all over the world. The air was thick with the sweet scent of fresh cow dung mingling with burning incense and the rich aroma of ghee from temple lamps—mhm!

I indulged in wonderful, healthy food—traditional Indian rice dishes alongside delicious vegetarian creations of fresh fruits and salads. Among the vendors selling clothes, jewelry, and other goods, I met fascinating people—Kashmiri traders, Westerners who had made Tiru their home, long-time regulars, and fellow explorers like myself, all drawn to the mystical energy of this sacred place.

My experience at the Ashram of SRM was deeply ambivalent. Nestled within an expansive estate at the foot of Arunachala, the Ashram provides living quarters for both Ashramites and visitors. Towering ancient trees offer shade to all while a playful clan of monkeys roams freely among them.

As you enter through the main gate, located along the town's main road, you are expected to leave your footwear behind. A massive, ancient, gnarled tree—acting as a guardian of the temple—spreads its umbrella-like canopy in welcome. Just beyond, the library awaits, filled with a vast collection of literature and wisdom.

From there, the sacred temple space unfolds along a pathway that reveals the peak of Arunachala and an eternal lingam burning just in front of the temple entrance. The meditation hall is always occupied to some degree, filled with visitors seeking stillness. Hoping to experience a moment of silent meditation with SRM, I assumed my posture—only to soon realize that many people around me, mostly Indian visitors, were chatting loudly on their phones or even having a kind of picnic within this sacred space. Meanwhile, SRM's eternal presence, crafted in shiny metal, continued to offer His gracing Darshan, untouched by the distractions around Him.

After a while, I quietly removed myself and wandered off in search of a more serene and revered spot. My feet led me outside the Ashram onto the path ascending the Sacred Hill. Yet, still within the Ashram boundaries, I encountered a regal being—a snow-white peacock standing right before me! I was mesmerized. What enchantment she radiated! Pure grace, beauty, perfection—her presence exuded dignity as if she were from another realm—butterflies flitted by, adding their own touch of magic. A little further along, behind a fence, I spotted the Goshala, the enclosure for the sacred temple cows. These majestic white beings, with their distinctive neck humps and deep, soulful eyes, seemed like Rishis in their own right—wisdom embodied. I felt truly blessed to have crossed paths with such divine beings.

Suddenly She Was There behind Me as I Strolled through the Ashram Garden

Arunachala Mountain is awe-inspiring, but my most profound spiritual experience of bliss occurred during a weekend workshop led by "Krishna" Ayya. He shared powerful insights and techniques that transported me into a deep state of ONENESS with ALL—a blissful connection that dissolved all boundaries between myself, Arunachala, and the entire world. I felt an overwhelming urge to dance, to embrace everyone and everything in my path! It was so effortless, so natural! I remained in this elevated state for the rest of my time in Tiru, and from that moment on, TIRU has held a sacred place in my heart. Thank you, TIRU, for the incredible gifts you bestowed upon me! I will return again. It is unfortunate that all the photos I took on this journey were lost, yet the memories remain deeply embedded in my soul.

Later, I spent some time in Chennai with followers of Patriji. However, I was taken aback by the sheer number of hospitals I saw. What had happened to Ayurveda? Was it no longer practised there? And why did I encounter so many ill and lost souls? What was going on?

Back Home to Egypt

Back in Cairo once again, I took on the task of cooking for the boys while Madhu was in India. However, I felt the need to move on soon.

Siwa, the westernmost oasis—this magical haven surrounded by the Great Sand Sea—had once enchanted me. Yet, after my third visit, I found myself repelled. Though I had met many wonderful locals, the increasing influx of Egyptians bringing with them distorted views of Western women had begun to taint the place.

The Siwi people, an Amazigh tribe and part of the greater Saharan Berber nation, are fascinating. With African roots, their traditional ways differ significantly from those of contemporary Egyptians. Brotherhood exists there, too, and some among them are highly educated, embodying reason and dignity—if only it weren't for the pervasive gender biases.

Meanwhile, drug and arms trafficking between Libya and Siwa led to the rapid decline of the region's beautiful traditions. The Egyptian Revolution had already cast a shadow over life everywhere, making matters worse. And so, I decided to give Luxor another chance, remembering my promise—to live there and, ultimately, to die there.

Siwa's Magic

More Meandering: Siwa/Luxor Once More

I moved all my belongings and settled back into Hagag's house, this time in a brand-new flat in the basement. It felt like a homecoming in more ways than one. Many people remembered me well, and I immediately felt at home. I started rebuilding my life, sharing the practice of meditation with anyone interested—completely free of charge. To my surprise, a large group gathered for our first meditation session at a hotel near the Nile. I was thrilled. The next session was set to take place on a felucca, sailing down the Nile. Once again, about twelve people joined.

We set off from the dock, sailing gently—an experience that was healing in itself. Everyone was deep in meditation when, suddenly, a loud crashing sound jolted us back to reality. The boat came to an abrupt halt, struck heavily on all sides. I opened my eyes and saw that we were surrounded by other boats. What was going on? Just as swiftly, the boats untangled themselves, each going its own way, and we made our way back to the dock.

As I stepped off the boat, I found myself alone with my Shunyata, my beloved instrument that I played during meditation. The others walked ahead without looking back or saying goodbye. What was happening?

Later, I discovered that the police had called one of the participants, demanding to know what we were doing. So, that was the situation! The authorities even questioned Hagag, my landlord. Fortunately, since he had known me for a long time, he truthfully vouched for me, saying only positive things. The police then instructed him to take a photo of us meditating and show it to them. Apparently, meditation was considered a suspicious activity!

But I refused to give up. People who do not have the courage to confront me directly are not dangerous—they're just scared. After that, they left me in peace. In fact, some local men even started joining our sessions, though I soon realized that many were more interested in me than in meditation! To make matters worse, even the women gave me trouble.

Faced with all these challenges, I decided to shut my doors for a month—to retreat within myself and uncover the deeper reasons behind these trials.

Turning To Myself Again

In September 2015, I lay down, allowing my entire body to rest, and let whatever wanted to surface from within reveal itself clearly. What was still at work inside me, drawing so much negativity into my life? Once again—for what felt like the thousandth time—I connected to the feeling of guilt, the relentless sense of never being good enough, no matter how hard I tried. Despair gripped me. I surrendered to it, releasing all control.

Tears welled up, and I began to cry. My entire body trembled under the weight of the pain in my soul. I sobbed and sobbed until the tears ran dry, until I was exhausted, utterly depleted—emptied out, lifeless, drained. And then, I rested.

From the depths of that emptiness, a deep sense of peace and serenity emerged. It flowed gently through my entire being, washing over me like cool, cleansing water, purifying every trace of pain. Ah, yes. And then, suddenly, a surge of fiery energy coursed through me, filling me with an electrifying exuberance. I felt radiant, blissful—reborn. A desire to sing, to dance in the streets, to embrace everyone overwhelmed me. I observed the entire process in awe, detached from any sense of time. What a rollercoaster of emotions! I had been carrying all these energies within me. Now, I felt completely renewed, as if I had been born again. Gratitude swelled within me.

This picture below shows the transformation.

Emotions are the messengers of our soul. They must be fully felt—all of them. They have the right to be expressed, guiding us toward healing and wholeness. When suppressed, they linger in our subconscious, causing unnecessary suffering both within and around us. In ancient African tribal cultures, rituals were practised regularly to release emotions in a structured, guided way. Emotions must be acknowledged and understood—they are the very essence of life. We share them not only with one another but also with animals and plants.

Yet, I also know that emotions arise in their own time, according to the script written in the book of my soul. The key is to relax, step aside, and allow life to unfold naturally.

In October 2015, a retreat was taking place in Dahab, organized by Ram, with Patriji as a participant. On impulse, I asked them to grant me an hour during the retreat to lead a meditation and share a short talk. I decided to take a leap of faith—to leave Luxor, vow or no vow, and give Dahab a chance. Bravely, I stood before an audience of around 40 people, sharing my deeply personal journey. I had no idea how my words were received—except for a few people who offered polite but surface-level responses. Did anyone truly understand?

Regardless, I was soon offered the opportunity to guard a guesthouse in Dahab for a minimal rent—an ideal arrangement, considering my depleted finances. And so, I decided to give Dahab a try.

Dahab – St. Catherine

Dahab was my next field of experimentation. I knew it had long been a hippie hideout, attracting young people from all over the world for beach life, diving, snorkeling, and water sports. Yes, I wanted to work with young people and those exploring the spiritual aspects of their lives. Perfect.

Full of fresh enthusiasm, I settled into a guesthouse that needed a thorough cleaning and clearing on all levels before I could begin. Once ready, I offered meditation sessions, a weekly kids' group, regular women's moon gatherings, and healing sessions. Things ran smoothly—for the most part. However, issues arose with the house owners and their Egyptian manageress. Again, I became aware of my obsessive sense of over-responsibility, taking on far more than was mine and expecting acknowledgment and respect in return. That never happened. Finally, I let go of this pattern, limited myself to what was expected of me, and started prioritizing my own interests.

By 2016, my father's health had deteriorated. I wanted to be with him, but my brother refused to send me a ticket, and I was broke. On March 20, 2016, I received the news of my father's passing. No one from our family had been by his bedside in his final moments. That pained me deeply.

On May 9, the inheritance came through, and my share was on its way to my account. This was, of course, a relief, as the ladies managing the guesthouse had decided to get rid of me. Generously, they gave me until the end of the month, but now I had the means to leave whenever I wanted. And I did—immediately.

I traveled to St. Catherine, in the heart of South Sinai, and spent a heavenly month in the sacred stillness of those towering mountains. Another new beginning was unfolding. Thank you, CosMa!

To the Left of the Cypress Trees Is "My" Little Rock House

There, in Wadi Shreeg, I found a charming little rock house perched on an elevated ledge overlooking a lush, green garden. The stillness was profound. I gave the owner some money to build a bathroom, install electricity, and paint the interior nicely. It was the perfect spot for a future retreat.

This place was near the Monastery of St. Catherine, home to the legendary burning bush that had appeared to Moses. I had no interest in it. To me, he was a traitor—one of those who had promoted the idea of a single god as a revolutionary concept. Was this another of Shivji's divine illusions?

For now, my priority was clear: I wanted to spend a month in an Ayurvedic retreat center in Kerala, South India. So, I did just that. The day after my inheritance landed, I booked the retreat. I also purchased a return ticket that allowed me to extend my stay if I wished. Done.

India Again: Udayagiri Ayurvedic Rejuvenation

My experience at the retreat center was truly enriching—let me share it with you! On June 25th, I landed in Calicut, a coastal city in Kerala, Southwest India. The thick tropical air enveloped me as palm trees swayed in the warm, soothing breeze.

From there, we embarked on a journey of several hours to my destination. Udayagiri Retreat is nestled high in the mountains, surrounded by untamed wilderness where tigers, elephants, monkeys, buffaloes, and snakes roam freely. The area is also known for its sprawling coffee farms. Once we left the city behind, the road wound through the jungle, offering me ample opportunity to admire the lush greenery. As we ascended, the mountain on which Udayagiri is perched came into view—partially hidden by dense foliage.

The final stretch of the journey was a bumpy ride as if the road itself was shaking us free of whatever we needed to leave behind. The air grew damp, clouds hung low, and a chill settled in at an altitude of over 1,000 meters. When we finally arrived, I was welcomed with warmth and kindness. My luggage was carried up a steep staircase, but before entering, I had to stoop low to pass through the doorway—a reminder of the value of humility. From that moment, I knew I was stepping into a sacred space.

I was assigned a room, though it didn't quite match my expectations based on the photos I had seen online. However, I was promised a different one as soon as it became available, so I decided to accept it for the time being. As I took in my surroundings, I was eager to explore the place where I would be spending my rejuvenation retreat. Let me show you some photos:

Thick Bushes All Around

View from My Room over the Land, Its Rainy Season, Best Time for rejuvenation!

My Humble First Room

Despite the uninviting room and the unexpected damp chill—temperatures hovering around 20°C or even lower—everything else was impeccable. The Ayurvedic doctor was exceptional, and the treatments were simply divine. Every single day, I was pampered for over two hours! The food was absolutely exquisite—so much so that I must show you the kitchen:

Freshly prepared foods were served with an abundance of love and prayer, offering a variety that was both simple and incredibly healthy. Of course, everything was purely vegetarian and made with the highest quality ingredients. Before long, I began to feel the harmonizing effects of the food—not just on my body but most profoundly on my mind! It deepened my understanding of the saying, You are what you eat! Everything is energy, vibrating at a certain frequency. Frequency—frequency—frequency—it echoed within me.

Mealtimes were shared with other guests in a beautiful, round dining area that overlooked the valley below. Often, a gentle mist drifted over us, adding to the serene atmosphere.

Sundays were extra special—meals were served on banana leaves, and the food was absolutely delicious! The guests came from all over the world, and each one of them was wonderfully kind and warm-hearted.

This Plate Is Nice & Full!

View from the Dining Area on the Balcony

The service was truly exceptional! Every wish was granted effortlessly, always accompanied by bright, welcoming smiles. It was a joy to receive such care—I felt pampered beyond anything I had ever imagined, and it was simply amazing!

Each day, I saw the doctor and received a variety of therapeutic massages—some with different oils, others with powders, herbs, and even onions and lemons mixed with turmeric and floral petals. I underwent nasal cleansing, eye and ear cleansing, warm oil massages, steam treatments, body scrubs, and daily medicated full-body baths. The doctor prescribed oral medications and customized my diet accordingly.

The highlight for me was Shirodhara—a steady stream of warm oil poured onto the third eye. Wow! I never wanted it to end. It transported me into such a deep, blissful state that I wished I could stay there forever! That's how much I loved it.

Every morning and evening, in the hall shown below, we practised Agni Hotra mantra meditation at sunrise and sunset, followed by Pranayama and Yoga exercises.

Our Agni Hotra & Yoga Space

The yoga teacher was a sweet young guy, but he bellowed his instructions so loudly and with such exaggerated emphasis—like relaxxxxxxxxx, inhaaaaaaale, exhaaaaaaale—that I eventually quit his classes and started practising yoga on my own in my room, on the bed. Believe me, I'm not exaggerating! I even tried using earplugs, but his voice still thundered through them! Hahaha.

This Is How They Beautify the Place Every Day

This Is How Elaborate the Locks on the Doors Are Crafted!

One day, we ventured out on a jungle safari in a jiggly, jouncy jeep and saw plenty of elephants, monkeys, and one enormous bird. But the elusive tiger refused to reveal its majestic, powerful self to us—at least, not until later!

My Two Favorite Ayurvedic Masseuses.
I Love Them and All the Other Lovely Flowers, too.

All in all, my 30 days in the jungle of Udayagiri were worth every penny and so much more. We transformed into a family in no time—staff, guests, workers, doctors, and everyone in between! A heartfelt thank you to all for your selfless, untiring, loving, and caring service. Keep up your amazing contributions to spiritual and holistic health; they are priceless, timeless, and, now more than ever, deeply needed.

It seemed that everything in India is done with a celebratory spirit! This love for elaborate décor is not just about aesthetics—it certainly catches the eye with its beauty, but there is a deeper energy within it all. It nourishes the soul!

Allow me to delve a little deeper into Ayurveda. The term itself is Sanskrit and translates to knowledge of life. It encompasses all aspects of nature, both within and around us. An Ayurvedic doctor first interviews the client to assess their state of being. Based on the chosen program—whether rejuvenation, detoxification, stress management, weight management, skincare, wellness, monsoon rejuvenation, Ayur-yoga treatments, or others—and the time frame, the doctor then designs a personalized regimen. This includes a sattvic diet with carefully selected herbal medicines harvested from pristine forests and processed using ancient recipes. The program also integrates yoga, daily Agni Hotra ceremonies at sunrise and sunset, and a series of body treatments that evolve over time to restore harmony and health. Even the seasons have a profound impact on the body and the healing process.

The treatments themselves are nothing short of extraordinary. Various oils, prepared according to ancient methods in perfect harmony with nature's laws, are used to restore balance. Each day includes a consultation with the doctor, who guides you step by step toward deep well-being.

We were even given a glimpse into the ancient alchemical processes used to create herbal medicines, which left a lasting impression on me. The strong scents of herbs and flowers play a vital role in enhancing the healing process. Moon phases also influence treatments—every aspect is performed with a profound understanding of and alignment with nature's cycles and forces. As I write this, I find myself longing to return to Kerala for another month of rejuvenation!

Ayurveda is an ancient, time-tested scientific system that realigns the body with nature and the soul within us. It is likely the oldest recorded, all-encompassing natural healing system on the planet.

Victory to Ayurveda! Victory to the Vedas!

Ashram of Paramahamsa Nithyananda

The last day had arrived, and it was time to pack up and bid farewell to my newly found, kind-hearted family in Udayagiri. A new adventure awaited—one I had long anticipated. I had been eager to visit Paramahamsa Nithyananda, a globally revered Enlightened Master at the time. I had watched his YouTube videos and listened to his profoundly transformative satsangs.

Back in Mexico, my German friend Angel had once handed me a tiny piece of paper with his name written on it, casually suggesting I check out his videos—nothing more. Out of curiosity, I did. Just listening to him speak made my mind feel clearer, lighter, and brighter. It was then that I realized just how much clutter I had been carrying in my thoughts. Now, it was time to take the plunge!

I discovered that the ashram was only a six-hour drive from the retreat center. Without hesitation, I enrolled in a weekend program. Everything had aligned so smoothly—almost effortlessly!

Swamiji Paramahamsa Nithyananda Aadheenam in Bidadi, Karnataka, South India

So, I set off to visit the ashram of this Enlightened Master—one who was ALIVE in the present! My beloved Sri Ramana Maharshi had certainly been an incredible presence, but he was no longer embodied, and that made a difference. I felt excitement mixed with a tinge of fear—or perhaps, more accurately, awe—at the thought of facing Paramahamsa, which means "Supreme Swan" and Nithyananda, meaning "eternal bliss."

Heading northeast through Mysore toward Bangalore on a bustling road, we eventually veered off onto a rugged path leading into a rural landscape. Winding through a small village, we finally arrived at a grand entrance flanked by radiant stone deities on either side. Security was tight—no taxis were allowed beyond the gate. I had to drag my heavy trolley myself. Swallow! My trolley was now stuffed with Ayurvedic goodies, making it a formidable challenge on the uneven, muddy dirt road. And to my dismay, there were no gentlemen around to offer help. Udayagiri's comforts were over—it was back to doing everything myself!

Grumbling but determined, I wrestled my trolley over the long, bumpy path toward the welcome center. By the time I arrived, I was sweating and panting!

Inside the welcome center, the pace was noticeably different—efforts to register and allocate guests to their rooms were somewhat scattered, though carried out with plenty of smiles and good vibes. After several hours, everything was finally sorted.

In the ashram, photography and videography were strictly prohibited. So, dear readers, you'll have to take my word for it! But worry not—the web was brimming with content: nithyananda.org. There is plenty to explore, and I have so much more to add!

I enrolled in a weekend webinar titled Conquering Life. Finally, the moment arrived. I entered the large hall called Nithyananda Sabha, where all major public events took place. Most of the attendees had followed the priests to the temple for Paduka Puja, leaving the hall nearly empty.

I sat down, innocently tuning into the vibrations. And then—woah! The floodgates burst open, unleashing an ancient torrent of pent-up energies. I was completely overpowered, a mere witness to the overwhelming force. What's happening? I wondered. And then, deep within, a realization dawned: I am home! The search was over. This was it. I had arrived where I belonged, where I was meant to be.

I had anticipated such a possibility, but now that it was actually happening, it felt surreal. Then, the mind—oh, the restless mind—took over, filling my head with distractions. Eventually, Swamiji came on stage, and with his presence, another flood surged—this time, of tears. When they finally subsided, I found myself retreating into my habitual arrogance—arms crossed, mind sharp and critical, ready to fire its arrows of resistance: Don't come near me. I've got it all figured out. Fear crept in. I was losing control of what I thought was my space. No! Hold on!

For the next couple of weeks, my journey in the ashram oscillated between surrender and resistance—immersing deeply one moment, then retreating in fear the next. By the end of August, after significant inner work and countless realizations (even though I had convinced myself long ago that I was already "done" with all that—ha!), a profound shift occurred.

Finally, I could face Swamiji with open eyes and an open heart during Darshan—that divine moment of receiving an energy gift through his deep, loving gaze and an accepting embrace. And then, the truth revealed itself. The barrier that had imprisoned me in the basement of my own soul for decades had a name: Guilt. Shame. Self-doubt. Self-hatred. Self-denial. Not good enough. This was how I had seen myself, judged myself, tortured myself—robbing myself of so much goodness.

But existence, in its infinite mercy, allowed the shift to happen. Gradually, joyfully, I began climbing out of that dark basement—not without first confronting the shadows that had lurked there for so long. As I shone the light of truth into their hazy eyes, they dissolved. And I emerged freer than ever before.

The factors that unlocked my inner space included:

- The Presence of the Enlightened Master – His powerful energy transmissions played a crucial role in my spiritual awakening.
- His On-going Teachings – Rooted in the ancient Vedic science of consciousness, as expounded in the Upanishads and Agamas since time immemorial.
- The Pure Ashram Life – A disciplined environment enriched by sattvic meals, morning yoga, daily pujas, and sacred ceremonies that connect us to the divine and elevate our frequencies.
- A Joyful Community – Individuals from diverse backgrounds and cultures, united in living the non-violent Advaitic life of yogis, dedicated to serving the Master and his grand mission.

Between programs, I felt the need to step away from the Ashram and take some time for reflection. So, I booked a stay at a very special hotel. The price was equally special—so much so that I regretted it almost immediately and attempted to cancel. However, I soon discovered that I would have to pay a portion of the fee regardless, so I decided to go through with it. I justified the decision by reminding myself that this journey was about reconnecting with myself and indulging in special treats—yes!

I spent six nights in that lush, serene garden, savoring delicious, healthy, and yes, ayurvedic food, prepared exclusively for me since I was the only guest. I relished the impeccably maintained, tranquil rock house, built in the traditional Karnataka style, adorned with intricate details that delight the senses and inspire an appreciation for beauty. The service was warm and attentive, leaving nothing to be desired.

One day, I discovered a ping-pong table in the garden, so I invited the young waiter for his first-ever ping-pong match. It was great fun! It got my body moving after so much sitting in the Ashram and made me feel alive again.

Here is the restaurant at Angana—a perfectly harmonious blend of color and design, both rustic and stylish. And this was the Courtyard, where my room was upstairs behind the round window—look, it's still smiling!

Each day, I embarked on adventurous motorbike trips with the young waiter to a nearby village to withdraw 10,000 INR from the ATM to pay for my stay. (It was during the demonetization period.) These trips also gave me the chance to explore the local market and browse the shops, adding an extra layer of excitement to my time there.

After six wonderful days at Angana The Courtyard, I took a hired taxi back to the Ashram. It wasn't far—just about an hour's drive.

I then immersed myself in the 21-day Nithyananda Yoga Teacher Training at the Ashram, fully embracing the yogic lifestyle. Some aspects came naturally to me, while others—like surviving on no more than two hours of sleep—were a challenge. I simply couldn't do it. Managing five hours was an achievement in itself, considering I had always been a solid eight-hour sleeper. I was willing to push my limits, but not overnight! Eventually, the training ended, and many of us left without the Acharya certificate. The standards were undeniably high!

NYTT Trainees under the Banyan Tree

Next, I had to leave India to renew my visa, as I had spontaneously decided to stay for the "Inner Awakening" program. On August 31, I flew to Colombo, Sri Lanka—a little paradise just south of India. I checked into a quaint hotel called "Saffron," where I was warmly welcomed by the most charming couple. Their small but pristine retreat, nestled along a river and surrounded by a lush garden, was perfect for me—a true nature enthusiast! Here she is, Dilrukshi, with the Buddha in the background and the Lotos in the garden.

Everything in Life Is Auspicious!

It was a remarkably quiet spot in the midst of a bustling modern city. I have an exceptional intuition for finding the perfect hotels! Sri Lanka had already crossed my path once before, in Berlin, where I had a little boy from Sri Lanka in my kindergarten class.

I befriended his hospitable and kind-hearted parents, often enjoying their company. They once invited me to the Sri Lankan Embassy on a public day, where I absorbed all the fascinating information shared, indulged in delicious food, and admired the cultural presentations. I fell in love with Sri Lanka.

To my surprise, the drums and dances I witnessed there bore striking similarities to those I had experienced in Nigeria among the Yoruba people. It reinforced the idea that the Indian subcontinent was once part of the African continent!

I returned to Bangalore on September 19 with a fresh visa and immersed myself in the "Inner Awakening" program at the Ashram alongside around 200 participants from all over the world. This program offered a profound deepening of the inner cleansing process and a recalibration of our cognitions, drawing us closer to our pure, core Self. As a result, we began manifesting third-eye powers on a massive scale. I was astonished at what I could do, all thanks to Swamiji's initiation of these powers within us. The "Inner Awakening" program serves as a gateway to revising our old mindsets and downloading a fresh, pure, and eternal consciousness.

This entire program was a deeply transformative experience, and I am profoundly grateful for everything I learned and encountered—the blissful people I connected with the abundant and delicious food I indulged in (without gaining weight!), and the powerful ceremonies filled with sacred mantras. The Rudra Abhishekam on Monday mornings and the homa rituals were truly awe-inspiring, leaving me in a state of boundless bliss.

I am now part of Swamiji's vast Sangha, blessed with the opportunity to travel, teach, and heal. And so, it shall be.

Gratitude—endless gratitude to Swamiji!

He enabled me to:

- Let go of resistance – I dropped the obnoxious "NO" to life, people, situations, challenges, and opportunities. I no longer resist; the tantrum-throwing child within me has calmed. My inner door is now open.

- Release stress – I have freed myself from a tremendous amount of built-up tension.
- Make peace with my self-image, my world, and my perception of the Divine – I no longer fear the UNKNOWN, for now, I truly know!
- Open my heart to love – Love now finds its place within me—love for the Divine, the Unknown, and most importantly, for myself.
- Allow life to fall into place effortlessly – It feels as if Swamiji has been the earthquake that reshuffled everything, setting it all in the right order, proportion, and dimension.
- Embrace life with a resounding "YES" – This positive shift has rendered judgment and excessive criticism unnecessary.
- Relax into life and trust myself – I now claim my full right to BE exactly as I am—an embodiment of Beloved CosMahaDevi! I radiate this truth with authenticity, integrity, responsibility, and a spirit of enrichment.
- Hold myself accountable – No more foolish excuses or procrastination. My life flows easily and joyfully now.
- Transform even my facial expressions – This was the first change I noticed! It led me to love myself as I am. The subtle distortions caused by cynicism and sarcasm have given way to a sweetly relaxed grace and symmetry.
- See balance and harmony reflected in the mirror – I now recognize a playful kindness and goodness in my own expression. I love myself completely!

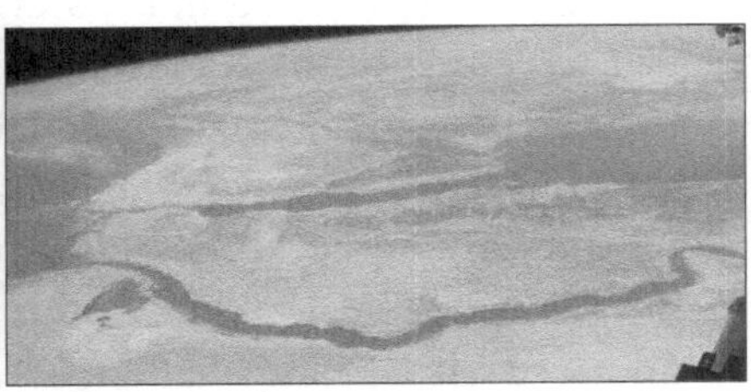

This Is Me Now! (left)
Sinai Peninsula – Red Sea – Nile (right)

Sinai/Dahab Again

After leaving the Ashram, I flew back to Egypt in mid-October 2016, searching for a future home in Dahab, South Sinai—a sandy strip of land between the Gulf of Aqaba and the Sinai mountain desert. The transformation was still unfolding, subtly continuing to clear and cleanse my inner space.

Dahab

Filled with enthusiasm, I set up my space with the intention of creating a Sangha, a spiritual community with the people of Dahab. However, this did not materialize on a larger scale, so I decided to return to the Aadheenam in Bidadi for another grand event—Sadashivoham 2016 in December. This experience turned out to be overwhelmingly chaotic. With 1,300 participants from around the world struggling with the effects of the on-going demonetization, nothing flowed smoothly; instead, we all faced significant challenges on a very physical level. I returned to Dahab sick and somewhat disheartened.

The Sangha still did not come together, and by the end of 2017, I moved back to Cairo. There, some workshops saw short-term success, but nothing substantial evolved. Disliking city life, I soon returned to Sinai, though by then, my financial resources were nearly depleted.

In 2018, I was gifted a four-month sojourn away from Egypt's scorching heat—on a beautiful Greek island, where life unmistakably nudged me to abandon my fruitless pursuit of money and instead turn inward, dedicating myself fully to my own spiritual evolution. From that point on, I spent my evenings watching YouTube videos of my beloved Advaitic Masters and teachers, absorbing their eternal wisdom deep into my being. This became my singular focus, apart from enjoying Greece's natural beauty and the kindness of its people. And I experienced that time and again, just before my purse emptied completely, something magical happened and it got filled again.

St. Catherine

Upon returning to Egypt, I moved to the sacred land of St. Catherine at the end of 2018, choosing to remain there and continue my inner quest for liberation. In doing so, I confronted the deeply ingrained and distorted perceptions of gender relations held by the local Bedouin community.

While there, I also found myself reliving a past existence—one in which I had been hunted, accused, abused, tortured, and ultimately burned at the stake, much like countless wise women during the Inquisition in Europe. We were a thorn in the eyes of the Roman Catholic patriarchs, who sought to shape society according to their own selfish and wholly unchristian designs. They thrived on fear and suffering—something that is becoming increasingly evident in 2024.

I faced these echoes of oppression among the Bedouins, who, in their own way, suppressed the power of women just as mercilessly. Yet, in that very place, I finally moved through and beyond my deeply embedded fears. Gratitude! From then on, I fully embraced the silent companionship of the towering mountains around me and cherished the priceless solitude that allowed me to immerse myself in my inner soul space. In that stillness, I danced with Spirit, Source, and CosMahaDevi in the depths of my heart—pure bliss and joy!

I reconnected with the essence of feminine consciousness—the deep, inner wisdom of natural interconnectedness. I invited this connection to grow strong and unwavering, for it is the ultimate state of being. These days, bliss flows over me—or is it flowing from within me? Yesssss! I am loving myself more and more each day. Finally, I have come full circle, back to ME! I did that decisive UI!

Victory to Women Power!

I felt as if I were truly birthing a completely new self—vastly different from the person I was when I first embarked on my soul's winding, serpentine journey.

I experienced how everything in nature held an open curiosity about me. The birds visited in the morning, chirping and tweeting their greetings. A fox, caught in the act of attempting to steal a chicken, paused to glance my way before sneaking off. A lizard scurried over, seemingly to inspect me, while the wind remained a steady companion, keeping the air crisp and cool—aaahh!

Life is so simple and easy, wallahi. What's all the fuss about, pipl? Just sit back, relax, and give thanks for the boundless riches that are freely given. Cultivate your garden, love your

neighbors, care for the animals, and water your plants. And above all, guide your children well—do NOT spoil them, or they will grow up spoiled, which means YOU missed the mark and messed up. Remember, you are a guest on EarthMa! Offer gratitude to CosMa always, in all ways, every single day.

I continued my sacred work of healing, clearing, and recreating myself on an even deeper level. A crucial part of this journey was gaining clarity about the significance of Swamiji, whom I had so dramatically encountered at his ashram in India. Through deep reflection, I realized I needed no outer guru—I had an inner Guide within my very own heart. I came to understand that the Source was Chitshakti, the Great Cosmic Mother, present within me as Her divine essence—CosMa. She had been with me all along, but I had to unearth Her presence beneath layers of old karmic imprints that had clouded my inner space. And lo and behold—only then could I truly develop trust, faith, and the unwavering certainty that I was loved beyond measure. It was a process, but with each passing day, I felt myself growing stronger and more stable in this realization. My outer experiences continued to affirm it, revealing to me time and time again that I was, indeed, loved and supported.

In 2020, I was gifted with a meditation practice that profoundly shifted my inner world—ZaZen. This practice, incredibly effective on all levels, allowed me to harness my entire being as an energy field, effortlessly eliminating distractions and dissolving distortions from my life. It also gently loosened any lingering ties to "religious" directives, as it embodied Buddha's guide to living in alignment with our original nature—free from fetters, rooted in our innate human goodness and compassion. My focus became singular: internal cleansing and on-going spiritual learning. I immersed myself in online teachings from evolved beings across the globe, drawing inspiration and remaining connected to a worldwide community of kindred souls.

The sacred silence vibrating within the ancient mountain giants at the heart of Sinai enabled me to dive ever deeper into my inner world. With utmost honesty, I faced and acknowledged the thoughts and emotions that had long sought recognition in the light of truth. It was so simple. And so easy—once I overcame resistance, confronted fear, and realized it was nothing more than a phantom in my mind. Just hot air. Pfpfpfffff. Meditation helped dissolve the false thought currents that roamed my mind, for they were NOT who I was!

I lived contentedly on my modest German pension, as life in Karina was affordable, simple, and grounded—just the way I loved it. Yet, I also enjoyed the "modern luxuries" of a flushing toilet, a washing machine, and even a four-burner gas stove. And still, my heart overflowed with joy simply for the immeasurable gift of being alive in a woman's body on this generous, loving, and beautiful EarthMa.

As time passed, the world plunged deeper into an unstoppable wave of chaos, transformation, and upheaval in 2020 and 2021. The peace I had found in my mountain solitude began signaling its inevitable end. I had felt it for some time—it was time to leave Egypt behind for good. Ten years had been enough. Moreover, my gifts found no receptive audience in a culture that had been in an internal lockdown for at least five decades, where deep-seated fears still held many captive. True openness requires courage, and courage was losing the battle there. The choice of freedom can never be imposed upon those too afraid to claim it.

As my farewell to this "land of light," which had offered me both wondrous and harrowing experiences—enriching me immeasurably—I leave you with this poem:

Egypt... Oh Egypt!

Just where are you heading?
You bid me to go now—that's what was seen and felt for a while.
Ten years, you have been my generous host,
You, once radiant jewel along the Nile!
You gifted me much healing in your city of a thousand palaces,
Deepened my understanding of communion with like minds.
You opened my feelings in the ancient round of Sinai giants.
I cleared all the muck in Karina's herb garden in their soothing, deep silence.
I am arriving back home now—where actually I never had left,
Just got myself enmeshed...
Yielding to the ONE—feeling myself much more solid and stable—
Ever sourced in that ONE.
My efforts to revive you were not well received,
So I left you to your fate to look after my own.

Farewell, ancient land! Gratitude for all your gifts,
Your beautiful people, amazing light, land of Sun Ra's radiance!
Who showers back rays of crystalline light at night...
I encounter Spirit face to face in your vast open spaces—
Your deserts all around, where heaven touches the ground.
Thick forests of Balah and Olive—oh, wonder
In the great sea of sand around Siwa.
Sleeping under your velvety skies, where your mind expands out of bounds,
Then, waking by the pigeons' gentle sounds...
Gliding down that vein of life on a silent white sailboat—Dahabeya—
A heavenly treat where time flies away...
Meditations in the King's Chamber, Giza, where initiation still goes on...

Fellahin tilling the soil in rhythms,
In a thousand-year-old simple way:
Four generations working as one.
And the fields change color according to season.
Palms heavily pregnant with fruit in midsummer,
The dates in a radiant, fiery dress—just to impress!
Enjoying the beaches along the Red Sea, where the mind takes off
To leave you free and clear of sorrow—no thought of tomorrow!
There's just so much to explore and enjoy
On this ancient old land of light!
Mighty beings had crafted this grand civilization,
Which—as everything—had long met its end under our feet in the sand…

Sure is that you have nurtured me deeply in my bidding for TRUTH,
Made me grow strong, patient, so much more SELF…
Huge is the harvest I reaped while with you.
Thus, you reside in my heart—forever.
Be you blessed in this time of global trial—
May your people wake up from their unconscious slumber
And awaken you forward to a fresh, bright glory!
Acid-clean your brainwashed conscience,
Shine the light of TRUTH on it, as your famous ancestors did!
Revive your inner riches now—remember who, in truth, you are!
And end your pains and suffering!
Leave your recent past in the past—
You know that NOTHING lasts on this plane!

High time now to embrace a fresh new game as ONE human family,
Where ALL are equal—yet each one unique—
And all join forces to bring back PEACE to reign!
Where love goes around, all life thrives to blossom
In harmony and freedom!

We realize the profoundest TRUTH: that ALL is only the ONE—
Formless, nameless, faceless, unfathomable—
And we're here to play that HIGHEST game!

Gender's the hellfire burning your souls so you would release your smelly false ways
And begin to honor one another in freedom and equality!
END THAT WAR!
Send your generals on eternal vacation,
So you can breathe out of that unified freeze.
Soften down—imbibe all the blessings under your feet—in great abundance!
Dive into your hearts now—heal the old lies,
And hearken to the mighty global calling to
UNIFY!

Zaytoona, August 11./12./13., 2020

Kenya

In October 2021, I found myself in Nairobi, Kenya. Over the past three weeks since my arrival, immersed in an entirely different energy field and climate, I began to feel my body subtly relax. The scorching, oppressive Egyptian heat had finally loosened its grip on me, allowing me to breathe deeply once again—fresh, green air filling my lungs. I relished the presence of the towering trees surrounding me, the rich red soil of Mama Africa beneath my feet, and the deeply grounded energy of the local people—settled, peaceful, content, humorous, and even-paced, at least at first glance.

A different kind of stress began to lift—the constant tension of ever-present police surveillance, the persistent burden of male harassment, and the exploitation of "tourists," as all Europeans were perceived. The unspoken, ever-lurking fear that gripped the general public in my previous environment slowly dissipated. These dense, oppressive energies had weighed me down without me fully realizing it.

As I surrendered more deeply to myself, I became receptive to subtle frequencies of healing and feeling. My being felt lighter and more translucent, and my energetic field was open and free—wow. A profound connection intensified within me, aligning with the cosmic waves of love and light, igniting my own inner radiance. Yes, I was ready! The survival-based stress melted away—ah, what a relief! It felt as though I were being refueled constantly, my practice of spiritual connection re-established and deeply rooted once more.

Boundless gratitude overwhelmed me, day in and day out.

I stood in awe of the ever-expanding dimensions of my soul as past life experiences surfaced—both earthly and cosmic. It was undeniable: I am an unlimited spiritual being encapsulated in a time-bound physical vessel. Yet even this body—this sacred temple—is a miracle, a profound mystery reflecting the limitless cosmic order. As above, so below.

René Schwaller de Lubicz unveiled this understanding in his book The Temple of Man. He and his wife, Isha, spent 15 years exploring every nook and cranny of the Luxor Temple, revealing its profound secrets through his writings. What an immense Divine Intelligence must have designed life with such intricate interconnection—wow. And how generous it is to have imbued us, humans, with the potential of that same limitless cosmic mind. I wholeheartedly embrace this Divine inheritance.

In truth, my entire life's journey has been about clearing away the illusions—shedding the layers of falsehood accumulated over thousands of lifetimes—to open myself as a pure channel for cosmic intelligence to flow through, unobstructed. A luminous cosmic mind, operating through a heart of pure love, executing divine will in its own unique, individual way.

After all, a diamond only forms under extreme pressure.

And as I catch the translucent sheen in my eyes and feel the energy flowing through my being, I can truly declare: Yes! I am a jewel. I am a gem. I am a gift. Life is given to us so we may celebrate CosMa—Spirit, Source, the Universe—with mindfulness, compassion, joyous abundance, and bliss. Amen!

I now recognize that every winding step of my journey has served this singular purpose—to cleanse my inner world of old debris, to dare to live from the profound depth that this process has opened up. HERE. NOW.

Every painful emotional struggle, every distorted self-concept, and every misleading societal, religious, and political dictate that has steered us away from existential truth—all of it has served its purpose. Humanity has long grown through suffering and pain, but now, we can choose to evolve through conscious awareness instead. A-hey!

For so long, I resisted my own inner growth. I thirsted for knowledge, feeding my intellect and inflating my ego to embarrassing proportions—until, finally, in the paradise of

Mexico, I unlocked the inner dungeon and faced my "beautiful demons." Only then could all the profound knowledge I had gathered alchemize into timeless wisdom, nurtured by spiritual initiations from past lifetimes. This wisdom became the fertile soil for my rebirth—REFRESHED, REJUVENATED, PURIFIED.

The Universe embraces us all as we step into a new era—one of peace, joy, freedom, and unity. We are called to live wisely, guided by spirit, as ONE HUMAN FAMILY, just as we did in grand cycles long past. Life is a gift meant to be celebrated in full awareness, carrying us to an even higher level of existence in harmonious concert with our galactic brethren.

And So Are YOU! And YOU and YOU and YOU, too!

Realizing that LOVE is, in truth, ALL THERE IS—how profoundly liberating this is! Yet, to reach this understanding, we must endure immense struggle, confronting the demons of our fears head-on—and even learning to befriend them. We must also overcome both our internal resistance and the external fears that challenge our ability to embrace this truth.

But the reward for such bravery is priceless: a life lived with a wide-open heart and a peacefully awakened mind. This alone is the true purpose of human existence on Earth, for its benefits extend to the very reaches of the grand CosMa Chitshakti. And what promise does this great awakening hold for humanity?

See what the Grand Sage of our time, Sri Ramana Maharishi of Arunachala, envisions:

Last but not least, I must add my latest poem on love

*L * O * V * E*

Life – Open – Vulnerable – Energy
Eternal Essence of Life

Life – Open – Vulnerable – Energy
Eternal Essence of Life
LOVE is: listening from deep within your heart.
LOVE is: perceiving – with nothing set apart.
LOVE is: receiving others as oneself.
LOVE is: understanding how we inter-are
in this mighty web of CosMa….
LOVE is: your attitude of YES to life, as it is – as you are.
LOVE is: bonding without glue, caring without fearing,
Giving without want, sharing for the joy,
Playing just like kids, weaving hand in hand,
Perceiving pure & clear, receiving as in giving,
Always ever HERE.

LOVE is universal medicine with the power to amend.
LOVE is deep, natural, connected harmony.
LOVE is co-creating for the good of ALL.
LOVE is silent communion with all life forms
By the power of awareness of the cosmic web,
Connecting all life eternally—
Interdependent, interrelated, continuous.
The global culture of LOVE is seeded in each heart already.
Each moment yearns to meet us in our hearts.
LOVE is our original nature—cultivate and radiate it 24/7.
LOVE is mindful, fully present, and deeply aware.
LOVE says: I am here for you.
SPIRIT is LOVE.
It is that web weaving, creating, connecting, interacting,

Engaging, enriching, sharing, serving, playing together – as ONE.

- for we are all equal – yet each one unique -

SPIRIT comes first—
For she quenches our thirst for LOVE in abundance.

There is nothing new under the sun,
Yet every cycle dons a fresh dress.
As our human consciousness expands
And opens to higher vibrations,
It remembers the inherited powers of old,
Applies the ancient magic of alchemy,
Inviting the fire to burn our fears and untrue desires…
Pure, reborn, light as a feather—
Rising from the ashes of fetters,
The prison of false mind—
We now rise up to co-create paradise,
Where ego has no place and is utterly redundant.
LOVE is dissolving "I, me, mine" in selfless altruism.
LOVE is serving & sharing to operate as ONE!
LOVE is holding sacred ALL life forms.
LOVE is living from the heart, living as the heart.
LOVE is the superpower—ever sourced in the ONE.
LOVE is the language that opens all hearts/doors,
amending all that was broken before.
LOVE is the motor that moves us through life.
We search for it outside, yet bear it to the brim within.
LOVE is a woman's nature—
understanding, embracing, accommodating,
creative without limit in her giving
of herself and of life.
LOVE alone makes life worth living,
and we receive it by our giving.
LOVE is who we are in our deepest core—universal.
And LOVE is what brings forth our creative expression.
And—do you know that ALL emotions arise from LOVE,

vibrate with LOVE, and return to LOVE?
LOVE is understanding our commonality in everything
as one human family.
And as life flashes from each of us, nothing is destroyed.
Change is the constant here—
and something is forever…
Oh Mystery, oh Grace,
reveal Your Divine Face to me.

L I G H T – T R U T H – P E A C E - JOY - BLISS

21.3.2021, Zaytoona/23.8.2021 Cairo

Shifting into a completely different and breathtakingly beautiful energy field in Kenya, I found that healing could now take place within my body temple—so deeply in need of restoration. I surrendered to the process, trusting that ALL IS WELL—and only getting better. Yes! And GRATITUDE!

I was reminded of a profound truth I once read in a brilliant book long ago: our endless thirst for love is fully quenched the moment we discover, encounter, and recognize the Divine within. No human relationship can match the bliss that flows from Divinity itself. That state of complete fulfillment—purity, grace, beauty, and balance—is the ultimate gift. Ahhh, GRATITUDE!

I have found that ONE TRUE LOVE that SEES, RECOGNIZES, and ACKNOWLEDGES ALL of me and LOVES, SUPPORTS, NURTURES, LISTENS TO, and CARES FOR ME in the most magical, unimaginable ways. I have discovered the LOVE OF MY LIFE in my own HEART. Home—at last. What a precious gift! What grace! And now, I realized it was never truly absent; it had only been obscured by lifetimes of conditioned beliefs filling the inner space.

I must share the insights that profoundly deepened my connection with the Divine and freed me from limiting suppressive religious constructs. Swamiji explained the essence of Creation: G for Generation, O for Operation, and D for

Destruction—spelling GOD. In Hindu spiritual science, this is further extended to include D for Delusion and L for Liberation—spelling GODDL. This introduces an entirely different dynamic, one of transformation rather than a rigid cycle that merely repeats itself at the same level. Do you see? Then he revealed another truth: we are here to fulfill our desires, not suppress them. And ultimately, life is meant to be celebrated—with devotion and gratitude for the countless blessings showered upon us every day.

Oh, ancient Bharat—India—the land of uncountable Goddesses and Gods, each embodying Divine qualities and powers. The land where Divine drama unfolds through unparalleled epics like the Mahabharata and Ramayana. A land that has preserved the most ancient and complete science of life—recorded in the vast scriptures of the Vedas and Agamas—still alive and potent, even in our modern, misguided age. Victory, eternal victory, to the science of truth and reality as it is! Where decay and death are ever-present—yet so too are beauty and abundance, overflowing.

Paradise lives in my heart – I can never be apart from it.

Summary

Looking back on my winding path, the greatest treasure I hold in my heart is the limitless healing power and compassionate presence of Mother Nature. She has been my best teacher, healer, listener, guide, and soothing companion. She moves with overwhelming force! I LOVE EARTHMA!

My sojourn among ancient cultures—Africa, Egypt, India, and Mexico—is another precious gem. They remind me of the wisdom and depth I carry within. I LOVE HUMANITY!

Books have been invaluable diamonds, helping me remember, inspiring me to explore, and urging me to rethink, reconsider, shift my views, and deepen my understanding. Finally, my own and others' creative expressions have gifted me joy, wonderment, enthusiasm, delight, excitement, and awe at the limitless scope of our creative potential.

Yet, my most priceless diamond is the realization that I have pursued my own individual path through the dense thicket of the deeply delusive world—both around and within me. I acknowledge that my intuition is awake, keen, and alive, and it has always guided me well—except when I allowed the monkey mind to take over. Or should I call it a parrot? Perhaps a sheep fits better—baah, baah.

Beneath the sheep's skin, the lioness has been quietly but vibrantly alive. At long last, she dares to roooooaaaarrr—Sekhmet in action! And she is ready to stride forward for another 75 years—celebrating life, Self, EarthMaji, GODDESSji, Deviji—Yiihaa! 2099! AGE is liberation!

The monkey mind never stops producing ideas; they sprout, expand, and distract me from the ultimate question: "WHO AM I?" Then I fantasize about manifesting them, and suddenly, I'm hooked again! And so, back to square one: WHO AM I? Drop the idea!

Many times, life has blessed me by NOT granting what I asked for! Oh my, yes. Thank you, CosMa, for saving me from my own foolish desires! And then, some quietly acknowledged wishes unexpectedly come true, and I realize, "Oh yes, I did long for this! And now it is here."

Within me, a child admires beautiful things and people and wants them. But I have often found that many things I acquired ended up merely being collected, never used. Being ever on the move, I have given away so much, realizing I only wanted them for the sake of having them. Yet, parting with certain things—books, musical instruments, my artworks—still brings pain. Within me, two opposing forces wrestle: one that clings and another, far more dynamic, that constantly seeks movement. Restless monkey, wait until I catch you by your tail! Just when I settle, the monkey knocks again: "Hey, let's go! Let's move on!" Some realize their true Self without ever leaving their spot. I am certainly not one of them! Though this inner conflict has brought suffering, my mobility has gifted me endless experiences and a lightness of being. A rolling stone gathers no moss—hmm!

Now, life flows at an even more peaceful pace as I surrender to the sacred process of healing my body temple. I do what I must to finally offer my contributions to the world. I know WHO I AM, how to groom and maintain my energy frequency, and how to shine my cosmic light on all I touch—as a beacon of light, a messenger of peace, and a child filled with innocence and joy!

I am truly birthing a completely fresh new Self, vastly different from when I first began my soul's winding journey. WoW!

I vow to live and be lived for the benefit of all beings! A–hey!

I thank and bless every sentient being who has crossed my path—those who have taught me tough and sweet lessons alike, those who have made me experience both suffering and joy, even love. Life overflows with richness in this sacred dance between polarities—opposites that ultimately merge into ONE PARADOXICAL, UNFATHOMABLE, COSMIC REALITY.

My final poem must be here—for the gender issue lies at the deepest layer of our collective delusions. Balance, peace, and mutual joy are possible once more! And it all begins within each individual—female and male alike!

The Sweet–Bitter Battle

A woman—a man—the primal scission,
Yet Spirit is ONE in our final fusion.
So how does it go—this polar roller coaster at this end of old time?
Well, men are still obsessed with sex, while women crave to emotionally attach—this creates unhealthy dependency!
Hm—we have lost the deep understanding of our true natures,
Of yang and of yin, and we are exhausting our kind
By that power-over, power-under battle—
The root cause of ALL global wars, hot or cold, it's doomed to grind to a HALT!
The fact is: the women are the stronger gender!
And men had better surrender to that now
And take their true position—that of full respect for her abundant powers!
And women might dare to unfold them now—ALL!
And aspire to own every one of them—wow!
More to ponder: in your soul, you bear no gender.
There, you are both in one, potentially being a spark of SPIRIT!
So, know thyself, all, to prevent another fall.
Open your eyes to clearly see before you dive into ecstasy.
Clear your field of old patterns—that is what now really matters
In this potential play of bliss.
Embrace both masculine and feminine powers within,
And allow the natural attraction to flower into a much higher kind and power.
Allow the small death—the end of the rabbit—to transform into a great death.
Share ONE breath and melt—end of ego—aaaaaahhh.
Dive into Taoist Tantric dance,
Invite Spirit to carry you straight into heavenly bliss
By His mighty, sweet, ecstatic kiss!

Imbued with love and honesty, deep, true sharing of the heart,
And in dignity and grace,
This is the place from where our human race
Can then reach into heaven—a new paradise!
A-hey—be it so!

IsIs 2010

My Final Words

The greatest treasure I carry within my soul is my experience in the bush of Yorubaland in Nigeria—this great nation with its timeless, wisely ordered communal society. I feel it has so much to teach humanity about living a healthy, peaceful, and joy-filled life well beyond the age of 100—rooted in the natural continuum of family and community, in harmony with nature, and ever guided by SPIRIT/SOURCE/COSMA.

It is my deep-felt intuition that this is where we humans will, at last, rediscover our fulfilment, satisfaction, and the timeless joy of BEING WHO WE TRULY ARE—free, divine, and embodying pure goodness. Signs of this awakening are already appearing! We are stepping out of the smothering delusions of the human-made matrix on a grand scale. It is TIME!

As 2024 nears its completion, the world is being shaken out of complacent illusions into a fresh new beginning—yihaaaah—let's embrace it! Now, more than ever, it is a profoundly personal journey to uncover WHO YOU ARE IN TRUTH so that you may contribute selflessly to the collective, serving our inherent UNITY—ONENESS—UNISON! Let us explore what more we can create together, always guided by the lovelight of CosMahaDeviji Chitshakti—the Grand Cosmic Mother—the Eternal DAO!

I thank you, dearest readers, for receiving, reflecting, and digesting! Be blessed and blissful—and feel free to connect and communicate. I love hearing from you:

irena.steininger at gmx.net

IrenStis at proton.me

There is a website, still in the making, check it out: Atartum.eu

9 789347 397516

Printed at Repro India Ltd.